I0019910

Roman Zenner

Hypertextual Fiction on the Internet

Roman Zenner

Hypertextual Fiction on the Internet

A Structural and Narratological Analysis

VDM Verlag Dr. Müller

Imprint

Bibliographic information by the German National Library: The German National Library lists this publication at the German National Bibliography; detailed bibliographic information is available on the Internet at http://dnb.d-nb.de.

Cover image: www.purestockx.com

Publisher:
VDM Verlag Dr. Müller Aktiengesellschaft & Co. KG, Dudweiler Landstr. 125 a, 66123 Saarbrücken, Germany,
Phone +49 681 9100-698, Fax +49 681 9100-988,
Email: info@vdm-verlag.de

Produced in USA and UK by:
Lightning Source Inc., La Vergne, Tennessee, USA
Lightning Source UK Ltd., Milton Keynes, UK
BookSurge LLC, 5341 Dorchester Road, Suite 16, North Charleston, SC 29418, USA

ISBN: 978-3-639-02823-2

Contents

Contents

Contents

[...] The cashier left to get a price check and Dirk, continually fascinated with everything, leaned over the barcode reader and stared deep into its laserous interior.

There was a beep and the cash register displayed:

POET $0.25

Dirk blinked and stood up. Scott and I watched, kind of mortified at whatever Dirk was about to do, because we knew from experience there was no stopping him when he was in this condition. Dirk ran his finger over the glass window.

There was a beep and the cash register displayed:

HYPERTEXT NOVELIST $19.95

"Wow, Dirk," William sputtered, "in your retina you are still a poet but your fingerprints have mutated to become those of a hypertext novelist, for which you are worth considerably more..." [...][1]

---

[1] http://www.unknownhypertext.com/hard_code6.htm, accessed 25.04.05

1. Introduction

[I]n terms of literary theory, it is fair to say that the hypertexts we can observe today, from the novels published by Eastgate Systems to those freely available on the World Wide Web, operate well within the standard paradigm of authors, readers, and texts [...][18, p.78]

Traditional texts and hypertexts are not fundamentally different - actually they have more in common than is commonly assumed and thus can be analysed well within the parameters of established categories of literary theory. Therefore, it is striking that quite a number of theoretical treatises on hypertext refer to the 'revolutionary character' of this kind of writing, the 'amazing technological development' that lies behind it, and the 'almost miraculous convergence of postmodern literary concepts and hypertext'. Following their line of argument, the new text-form also had the potential to replace traditional printed literature almost completely. BOLTER, one of the first hypertext theorists, claims for instance that "[...] the printed book, therefore, seems destined to move to the margin of our literate culture." [24, p.2]. Successively, these enthusiastic and unrealistic assumptions are being questioned. INTEMANN for instance asks:

Ist Hypertext wirklich ein ergiebiger Forschungsgegenstand? Hypertext ist nichts Neues, sagen Kritiker, denn Verweisstrukturen gibt es auch in Lexika. Ein Inhaltsverzeichnis kann als Sammlung von Hyperlinks betrachtet werden, demnach ist jedes Buch zum Durchblättern ein *Hypertext*. [46, p.11]

1.1. Aims of this dissertation

Using a body of primary fictional texts reflecting the diversity of electronic writing, this projects aims at analysing hypertexts from a literary rather than a technologically oriented perspective. The purpose of this thesis is to use categories and analytical tools from literary theory, filter out their essence and shape them into what could be called an analytical toolkit for close reading of hypertexts. In a second step, then, I would like to apply these analytical tools to a set of primary texts which have been chosen for their variety and 'otherness' in order to cover a wide scope of possible variations.

1.2. The Problem

> Die Forschung hat ihren eigentlichen Gegenstand bisher weder phänomenologisch
> umrissen noch begrifflich genau gefasst und ist, was konkrete Fallanalysen betrifft,
> kaum die ersten Schritte gegangen. [81, p.25]

The academic study of fictional writing based on hypertextual structures and characteristics faces a number of problems. Firstly, although a plethora of different works of this kind have been published, *afternoon - a story* by author and hypertext-theorist Michael JOYCE is one of the very few works to date which have undergone a comparably close analysis. This is especially striking since it is more than ten years old, which in the modern age of global digital information, where the development of new technologies and ever-faster computers and connections can be witnessed almost daily, is indeed a very long span of time.

> The existing two dozen hyperfictions have been discussed in at least 300 critical
> texts, according to Richard Gess, an observer of the scene [...] This impressive
> ratio between literary production and academic discussion prompts me to label
> the discourse about hyperfiction "hypertheory", implying that the theory of hy-
> perfiction has become a genre in its own right. It is a parasitical and uncritical
> genre [...][75, p.312]

1. Introduction

In the same vein, PUROMBKA [68, p.320] argues:

> Wenn Bolter also mit *Storyspace* und *Afternoon* ein neues Zeitalter für das elek-
> tronische Schreiben markiert sieht, dann verweist er damit vor allem auf die eigene
> Leistung und auf die Leistung der *Storyspace*-Fraktion, zu der später noch der Li-
> teraturwissenschaftler George P. Landow hinzukommen wird. Seit 1987 bildeten
> Bolter als Medienwissenschaftler, Joyce als Autos, später Landow als Literaturwis-
> senschaftler und Marc Bernstein als Verleger zusammen ein schlagkräftiges Team,
> das auf allen Positionen gut besetzt war. Sie haben in Vorträgen, Aufsätzen,
> Werbebroschüren, Büchern und Hypertexten das Bild vom Hypertext bei Nicht-
> Informatikern, vor allem bei Geisteswissenschaftlern entscheidend geprägt. *Der*
> elektronische Netztext, der in den Bereichen Literatur, Literaturwissenschaft, Philo-
> logie, Philosophie gleichermassen einsetzbar war, der Leser ebenso wie Autoren von
> den Zwängen des Buches befreien sollte, ist deshalb jahrelang erst einmal eine Art
> *Storyspace*-Text gewesen.

Moreover, it is recognisable that existing critical literature on the subject is often
concerned with what could be termed "macrostructures" of hypertext, i.e. its overall
textual composition. Thus, the analysis of this type of literature is mostly performed on
a rather abstract level. In this respect, text-linguists have developed a range of descriptive typologies in order to be able to account for the new fragmented and networked
structures of hypertext.[1] These studies, however, focus more on the communicative aspects of texts and their potential for the organisation and transmission of information.
Texts that are analysed in this field are often non-fictional internet-pages, which are
scrutinised for their effectiveness. Not surprisingly, web-site usability research is closely
intertwined with this linguistic study of hypertext.

Finally, hypertextual fiction is not yet being supported by a broad readership, i.e. it
has not entered the literary mainstream yet. One of the results, beside others, is that a

---

[1]While researching the topic, I found that most academic work in this respect has been performed in
the field of linguistic studies in Germany.

canon of literary hypertexts has not yet evolved. As we will see, there have been several attempts at furthering broad acknowledgement of hypertexts. One is to have writing contests and literary awards. This procedure is based on the assumption that a) the works can be critically described and judged accordingly and b) it is possible to make them undergo the same processes as in the established world of print literature. Awards like these are for example the Trace/Alt-X award, the winners of which, for example *The Unknown* and *These Waves of Girls*, will be analysed in this dissertation.

History Hypertextual fiction has been produced since the middle of the 1980s, and numerous introductions and editions already write the literary history of this rather young field. For more detailed accounts I would like to point to the comprehensive overviews written by Marie-Laure RYAN [72], Ilana SNYDER [82] and Carolien VAN DEN BOS [25]. Here, the reader will find definitions and details concerning the development of the concept of hypertext of the field's 'grandfathers' Vannevar BUSH, Douglas ENGELBARTH, and Theodor NELSON.

In order to describe the history of hypertextual writing, we can broadly identify two major phases of development: In the first phase, which started with the publication of the first work of fiction written in hypertext, namely Michael JOYCE's *afternoon - a story* [11], there was a sense of overwhelming enthusiasm concerning the death of the printed book due to the seemingly indisputable advantages of electronic writing. Hypertext scholars such as George LANDOW even have gone as far as to enthusiastically announce the turning away from print literature towards the vast technical possibilities of interlinked electronic texts, a position that has been termed "technological determinism". More than a decade later, there remain only a few voices sharing this position. This latter phase is mostly characterised by scepticism towards the newly-evolving form of writing. Articles such as *When Hypertext became uncool* [97] or *Why Hyperfiction Didn't Work* [62] suggest a counterreaction against the enthusiasm of the early hypertext theorists, also referred to as "hypertheorists".

The first wave of literature on electronic textuality has been enthusiastically promotional: in the early days of the new medium, the most urgent task was to convince the public that there was a need for it [...] In a second wave, the hyperbolic promises of VR [Virtual Reality] and hypertext developers triggered skeptical counterreactions and passionate elegies to the Codex book. [73, p.16]

Fictional writing on the internet   The internet as a quickly developing network of interlinked computers, at least from the perspective of artistic text production, has not been taken account of in quite the same manner as traditional printed literature and CD-ROM hypertext. And while these internet hypertexts and their study have inherited all the problems from their 'older brother' offline-hyperfiction, there even are some additional ones to consider.

Firstly, there is a considerable discrepancy between the amount of close reading that is dedicated to traditional poetry and narrative and hypertextual fiction on the internet. Students of English, especially in their initial semesters, are usually taught how to identify figures of speech and patterns of meaning in various poems, and the narrative situation and the story/discourse dichotomy in short stories and novels. In comparison, if one can find a piece of criticism on a given work of hyperfiction, it will - analytically speaking - most certainly remain on the surface and rather stress the hypertextual properties instead of the literary ones. Here, we can identify a number of reasons for this state of affairs. One of them is that because of their very form the works in question are somewhat unstable and even ephemeral: They are not published in print or fixed on a CD-ROM, they have not got an international book number, and if the author decides to change or delete one or more files of his work on and from the respective server, the work as such is irretrievably gone. STORRER [84, p.12] also refers to this problem:

Im WWW müssen Autoren immer wieder überprüfen, ob die Module, zu denen sie einen Link gelegt haben, inzwischen nicht inhaltlich verändert, "umgezogen" oder gelöscht sind.

Nowadays, actions are being taken in order to prevent loss of these electronic texts, a good example of which is the *Electronic Literature Directory*. Another reason for the

1. Introduction

somewhat hesitant approaches to electronic writing on the internet might be that many scholars doubt that this new form is a potent basis for works of considerable artistic quality. In this sense, FAUTH [41] critically argues:

> Browsing the World Wide Web can serve as a quick antidote to the foaming eupho-
> ria proponents of hyperfiction foster. Most hyperfiction encountered here seems
> clumsy, unsatisfactory, and of little artistic merit. Once the novelty of clicking on
> underlined words or outlined icons wears off, there is not much left to be euphoric
> over – the stories seem to be lacking in everything but innovative structure, and
> the structures seem murky and pointless. There is a sense that the basic elements
> of the form have not been understood properly and are used in a haphazard way
> by most of its pioneers, happily experimenting on the fringes of cyberspace.

In the same vein, he argues that - quite typically of modern forms of art - artists relied too strongly on the innovative and additional means these forms provide and terms this the "poles-in-your-face"-effect:

> Many of the hyperstories found online are lacking in content and quality writing
> because the novelty of hypertext makes all other aesthetic concerns secondary.
> This seems to be an intrinsic problem with newly discovered forms or variants of
> forms – the same obsession with the possible explains why early stereo recordings
> commonly feature oscillating sounds between the left and right speakers and actors
> in 3-D movies tend to wield poles toward the camera. The special feature in a
> medium, at least during an initial phase of experimentation, tends to be overused
> while eclipsing other, more traditional qualities. [41]

Terminology   Another problem of the study of hypertext is the fact that although there is a variety of different technical terms, analytical tools and definitions, these seem to be rather vague in some respects and still need to be incorporated into a larger terminological and theoretical framework. Furthermore, it could be argued that hypertext-theory overemphasises the postmodern properties of these texts and neglects other strategies and tools of literary analysis.[2]

1.3. Method

1.3.1. Instruments

The aim of this project will be achieved mainly by setting up an analytical toolkit based on characteristics and classifications deriving from a broad and interdisciplinary model of narrative analysis. This model, thus, combining a variety of theoretical approaches, will then be tested by using its tools in close readings of various primary texts.

Some questions that will lead my analysis and serve as guidelines will be: 1) What tools do traditional methods of literary analysis provide for the analysis of hyperfiction? 2) Are these sufficient or do we need to expand/modify some of these to account for existing texts on the internet? 3) Does hyperfiction constitute a new genre?

As far as the development of this project is concerned, I would like to use the four criteria RYAN has set up in her introduction *Cyberspace Textuality* [72, p.16] as a guideline:

> What we need at this stage in the development of cybertext theory and criticism is neither wild promotion nor denigration, but (1) a critical, though not hostile, assessment of the claims of the first-generation developers and theorists; (2) a way to read the individual texts that finds a middle ground between pure description of the works and general considerations about the medium; (3) a poetics tailor-made for electronic textuality; and (4) a thematic approach that relates cybertexts and textual constructions of cyberspace to the major human, aesthetic, and intellectual concerns of contemporary culture.

---

[2]As will be shown, 'hypertext theory' is mainly based on assumptions and categories suggested by literary critics such as Roland BARTHES, Michel FOUCAULT, and Jacques DERRIDA.

It will become evident that the theoretical approaches one could list and use for the analysis of the texts in question are manifold, and it is needless to say that they cannot all be integrated into this presentation. For example, since the internet is a global phenomenon, using English as its primary language, we are in fact faced with a cross-cultural artistic background; interesting results, then, will also be gained from cooperation with the areas of comparative and cultural studies. Especially the latter, with concepts such as popular culture and sub-culture as well as the various definitions and implications of culture itself can certainly be connected to this project. Also, the group of texts which concern themselves with armed conflicts evoke the historical, political and social dimensions these texts have and which could also be followed. A thorough discussion of all interdisciplinary connotations is, of course, far beyond the scope of this presentation, and further research in these more specific areas may develop important contributions.

The preliminary model   This presentation, therefore, restricts itself to two main areas of interest. First of all, we will be looking at existing descriptive categories for hypertext, which are often found in secondary literature, eg. interactivity and non-linearity. However, rather than to conclude my analysis with these findings, I would like to deduce a workable model from these and ask questions such as "To what extent is the present work interactive?" and "Is non-linearity a crucial part of the narrative development of this text?" Secondly, I would like to refer to traditional tools of literary analysis and test them for their applicability to the new sort of texts.

1.3.2. Corpus

When looking for a suitable corpus of primary texts for my analysis, I was naturally faced with the problem of choice: since there are quite a number of hypertexts on the internet, I had to limit myself to including specific texts the analysis of which I hoped to be fruitful and relevant for the context of this research. Hypertexts reflect the common reading-mode of today's internet user: browsing rather than reading. The internet is normally used as a gigantic source of information, the retrieval of which necessarily has to be effective and thus very quick. Thus, webpages have to 'come to the point' rather quickly, otherwise the visitor would lose patience and turn attention to another source.

When selecting the individual works I have focussed on finding a broad variety of texts in order to be able to account for a significant portion of the spectrum of writing that exists today. In order to include works that are particularly relevant for the field of hypertextual writing, a good starting-point is to find contests and awards and highlight some of the winners. Although SHUMATE [78] argues that "[L]ooking to lists of contest and prize winners as a measure of quality in any artistic field is risky business [...]", he nevertheless concedes that especially for a young academic field such as hypertext fiction it is justified to focus on the awarded texts as "[...] a legitimate place to begin reading."

1.3.2.1. Electronic Literature Directory

There is a substantial number of works to be found in the directory of the ELECTRONIC LITERATURE ORGANISATION (ELO). According to the ELO, it is a "[...] descriptive guide to 2,280 works, 1,160 authors, and 181 publishers [...]"[3] from the area of electronic literature. ELO also awards outstanding works of modern electronic literature, and in 2001 for example, Caithlin FISHER has won this award with *These Waves of Girls.*

Another initiative of the ELO is its "Preservation, Archiving, and Dissemination project" (PAD):

> At the Electronic Literature Organization Symposium, The State of the Arts, held in April, 2002, at UCLA, writers, scholars, and teachers agreed upon a pressing need: a means to retrieve and preserve works of electronic literature from the ravages of technological "progress" that leave the works inoperable in new technical environments, and thus inaccessible. While these pioneering works promise to form a major part of the future of our literary heritage, their constant fading into technological obsolescence frustrates the formation of the critical and scholarly perspective required for that to happen. PAD envisions to preserving these works in forms that render them available to readers, supportable as part of museum

---

[3]`http://directory.eliterature.org/`, accessed 25.04.05.

collections, and suitable for scholarly research.[4]

Naturally, the creators of this directory had to develop strategies in order to make the vast amounts of information accessible and browsable. Here, KENDALL/TRAENKNER claim that the ELD "[...] attempts to resolve the unique bibliographic problems posed by the medium - problems that, if left unresolved, threaten to delay universal acceptance of new media writing, limit the amount of critical and scholarly attention it receives, and hamper the growth of its readership [...]" [52, p.1]. Apart from the broad categorisation of poetry/fiction/drama/nonfiction, which constitutes the first branch, the second branch, in contrast, refers to the overall quality and structure of the primary works in question and is thus titled *Technique/Genre*. Here, the editors of the directory offer definitions[5] as to what is actually included in the respective categories, i.e. how they have to be understood (cf. Appendix A.3). Without a doubt, this categorisation is the most comprehensive and most detailed approach found on the internet today and in my opinion reflects the enormous artistic scope of this medium. And while there is a certain degree of overlap, and works belong to more than one category, it still serves as a suitable guideline when one would like to approach these texts. Moreover, we can see that the categorisation is based on structural and technical features the respective texts have, and arguably, a content-oriented typology still needs to be developed.

For this research, I would like to restrict my choice of texts to the very first category - hypertext. The main reason for proceeding like this is the fact that in contrast to all other groups mentioned here, hypertext mostly relies on written text in order to transport information. Hence, having in mind to take a literary approach to these texts, hypertext fiction seems to be the obvious choice for inclusion into our corpus. Video and animation might be of more interest to film theorists, and generated-text experiments certainly provide an interesting field of discussion for linguists.

Other online-catalogs that make electronic writing accessible but do not share the

---

[4]`http://www.eliterature.org/pad/content/mission_statement.php`, accessed 25.04.05.

[5]`http://directory.eliterature.org/html/dirinfo.shtml`, accessed 25.04.2005

1. Introduction

ELD's comprehensiveness and browsing functions are the RHIZOME ARTBASE[6], the respective subcategories of the OPEN DIRECTORY PROJECT[7], and the YAHOO! directory[8].

1.3.2.2. Other Sources

Another strategy of retrieval is to make use of a search engine like GOOGLE or YAHOO and search for keywords such as 'hyperfiction' or 'electronic fiction'. Here, a large number of results containing both primary and secondary can be found.[9] Either one finds the direct internet-link to the works listed in the search-result, or one is led to pages which serve as portals to access a greater number of hypertexts. Also, there is quite a number of so-called 'e-zines', i.e. magazines and journals which are exclusively published on the internet, discussing issues of electronic fiction such as *Dichtung Digital*, *JoDI* or *Drunken Boat*. Furthermore, we can find many mailinglists (*webartery*, *rhizome*), newsletters (*Rohrpost*), forums (*Trace*) and newsgroups (*alt.hypertext*) which make it easy to spot a substantial amount of works as well.

It has to be noted at this stage that because of the sheer mass of primary works that exist on the internet today, any selection is bound to have at least a residue of personal preference. Even more so because conceptional and theoretical delineations do not seem to have been established in view of this genre yet, which could reasonably reduce the amount of primary texts. Thus, the primary subdivision will be made in view of the categories the creators of the ELD have used in order to cope with the amount of writing that exists today in the field of digital literature. Only when these texts have more closely been analysed, so that some genres could be isolated, will it be reasonable to approach these texts with a closer text-range in mind.

---

[6]http://rhizome.org/artbase/, accessed 25.04.2005

[7]http://dmoz.org/Arts/Literature/, accessed 25.04.2005

[8]http://dir.yahoo.com/Arts/Humanities/Literature, accessed 25.04.2005

[9]A search by the term 'hyperfiction' in GOOGLE yields about 49,500 pages (search performed 22.04.05).

2. Definitions and Categories

Digital literature is not yet an established genre. As a matter of fact the technical terms hyperfiction, hyperliterature, interactive literature, electronic literature, aleatoric text, cybertext, ergodic literature are used as synonyms or are not clearly defined semantically. Almost every scholar uses another, individual definition, includes certain aspects and excludes others. [69, p.15].

2.1. Electronic Literature

The phenomenon of electronic literature in its widest sense has provided us with a variety of terms and definitions that can partly be used as synonyms, and partly reflect special characteristics of the texts described. In the following chapter, I would like to create an inventory of these various definitions and filter out which of these can be used best for the purpose of this research. According to the creators of the ELD, the following definition applies:

> We chose to define electronic literature as work in computer-readable format that could not be published in print without sacrificing or altering significant elements that depend upon the electronic medium. A work must have one or more of the following to qualify for inclusion in the ELD: interactive elements, multimedia elements (audio, video, or animation), algorithmically generated text, or prominent visual elements. [52, p.2]

The term 'electronic literature', thus, represents an 'umbrella-term' for all texts that are published in a computer-readable format.

2. Definitions and Categories

Cybertext/Ergodic Literature   Norwegian scholar ESPEN AARSETH in his important treatise *Cybertext - Perspectives on Ergodic Literature* added some valuable insights to the discussion of hypertext in the late 1990s. Regarding terminology, AARSETH [18, p.1] defines 'cybertext' as follows:

> [Text which] focuses on the mechanical organization of the text, by positing the intricacies of the medium as an integral part of the literary exchange. However, it also centers attention on the consumer, or user, of the text, as a more integrated figure than even reader-response theorists would claim. The performance of their reader takes place all in his head, while the user of cybertext also performs in an extranoematic sense.

What is striking about AARSETH's work is the way in which the author does not right from the start establish the strict separation between printed and electronic texts and refers to works "ranging from ancient China to the Internet" in his analyses [18, p.65]. For him, the single most important characteristic is the overall ergodic quality:

> During the cybertextual process, the user will have effectuated a semiotic sequence, and this selective movement is a work of physical construction that the various concepts of "reading" do not account for. This phenomenon I call *ergodic*, using a term appropriated from physics that derives from the Greek words *ergon* and *hodos*, meaning "work" and "path". In ergodic literature, nontrivial effort is required to allow the reader to traverse the text. [18, p.1]

Ergodic texts and the different functions they are defined by will be discussed in detail later in Chapter 3.8.2. At this stage I suggest it suffices to note that AARSETH successfully 'tears down the walls' between electronic and printed texts.

Hypertext   The term hypertext was originally coined by Ted NELSON:

> By hypertext I mean non-sequential writing - text that branches and allows choices to the reader, best read at an interactive screen. As popularly conceived this is a series of text chunks connected by links which offer the reader different pathways. [64, p.2]

Similarly to AARSETH in the definition before, in this extract NELSON does not specifically refer to the electronic environment these hypertexts are presented in. His own research, however, centres around computers, which is also shown in his aim to establish a world-wide computer-network long before the invention of the internet. His vision has accumulated in what he has called the *Xanadu*-Project: a gigantic network of information accessible to everybody.

INTEMANN also presents a number of different definitions of 'hypertext', quoting various sources on her website:

> **Encyclopedia Britannica**: The linking of related pieces of information by electronic connections.
>
> **Oxford English Dictionary** Text which does not form a single sequence and which may be read in various orders; spec. text and graphics (usu. in machine-readable form) [...]
>
> **Ted Nelson** (1991): The best current definition of hypertext ... is 'text structure that cannot be conveniently printed'
>
> **Keep/McLaughlin** (1995): Hypertext is the presentation of information as a linked network of nodes which readers are free to navigate in a non-linear fashion.
>
> **Jakob Nielsen** (1995): Hypertext can only be done on a computer, whereas most other current applications of computers might just as well be done by hands [sic].
>
> **Nick Wiles** (1997): HyperText is a non linear document which contains nodes and links [...][1]

Her own definition of hypertext (or rather hypertextuality) will be discussed in detail in Chapter 2.3. For now, I suggest it suffices to propose that (electronic) hypertext is a text-form consisting of a number of textual fragments (lexias) which are interconnected by links.

---

[1] `http://www-public.tu-bs.de:8080/~intemann/hypertext/vortrag-hs/welcome.html`, accessed 25.04.05

2. Definitions and Categories

Multimedia   Multimedia today, it could be argued, describes the whole marketing concept of combining different sorts of information-transmission into one channel. Whereas before the development of electronic platforms and global networks these transmissions have occurred separately (films on television or cinema, music on radio, record or CD), we are currently witnessing a coexistence of these on modern computer systems. This combination of audio, video, and sound, together with a certain degree of interactivity and ways of jumping between these different modes, is usually referred to as being 'multimedial'.

> Nicht nur in der Öffentlichkeit, auch in der wissenschaftlichen Diskussion ist die Bandbreite dessen, was als Multimedia bezeichnet wird, erheblich. Der kleinste gemeinsame Nenner ist darin zu finden, dass Multimedia eine Technik ist, bei der Schrift, Ton, und verschiedene Arten von Grafiken (still, animiert), Filme (Trick, Dokumentation, Kunst etc.) oder virtuellen [sic] Umgebungen (Avatare, *Virtual Reality*) gemeinsam auf einer höheren technischen Plattform verfügbar sind und ein gewisses Mass an Interaktivität bieten müssen [...] [46, pp.67-68]

Related to 'multimedia' is the term 'hypermedia': Nelson's definition of 'hypertext' stemming from 1967 has been expanded later on and has become 'hypermedia': Here, in addition to the existing concept of 'hypertext', the importance of multimedia (such as audio- and videosegments) as well as nonlinearity is stressed.

Hyperfiction/Hypertext Fiction   This term is generally used to indicate that the technological development of hypertext is used for artistic purposes. Soon after the development of hypertext software, writers began experimenting with hypertext, creating new forms of fiction. Here, SUTER [87, p.28] offers the following definition:

> *Hyperfiktion* ist *demzufolge die literarische Ausformung eines elektronischen Textes mit Verbindungen, die den multiplen Zugang zu Informationen ermöglichen.* Eine Hyperfiktion ist also ein komplexes literarisches Gewebe, in welchem multilple [sic] (narrative) Abläufe durch die implementierte Verknüpfungsstruktur direkt sichtbar werden und der Leserin erlauben, ihnen nachzugehen. Eine Hyperfiktion kann

2. Definitions and Categories

verschiedene Stimmen und beispielsweise mehrere Perspektiven enthalten, die der Leserin zahlreiche Perspektivenwechsel ermöglichen. Die Leserin wird hierbei zum Mitgestalten der Fiktionen herangezogen, das heisst in Entscheidungsprozesse involviert, die den weiteren Verlauf der Fiktion bestimmen können. In den meisten Fällen werden also zwei Leserinnen einer Hyperfiktion nicht die gleichen Fiktionswege beschreiten, sondern sie werden zwei unterschiedliche Geschichten aus einer Hyperfiktion (heraus)lesen.

Thus, a number of important concepts and issues can be identified in this definition, which will be described and developed further in the ensuing chapters. The author describes 'multiple reading paths', a notion which refers to the narratological phenomenon resulting from the arrangement of text-fragments in an information space rather than a linear piece of writing.

As for the reading experience, Hilmar SCHMUNDT [75, p.311] suggests with reference to MOULTHROP's *Victory Garden*:

> The brevity of the text segments seems to emulate the disjointed superficiality of the post-industrial information society. No more than twenty lines of text appear at a time: replacement instead of synopsis, palimpsest instead of overview. Hyperfiction washes around the reader in echoes, ripples, and buzzed whispers of associations, instead of clearcut plots.

Here, it is instructive to note that the critic refers to the offline-type of hyperfiction: *Victory Garden* is also published and distributed on CD-ROM by American publisher EASTGATE.

Interactive Fiction According to SIMANOWSKI [81, pp.15ff], ZIEGFELD has coined the term 'interactive fiction' in 1989. Nowadays, this term almost exclusively refers to the world of a specific kind of computer games, e.g. adventure games. Usually, the player interacts with his counterpart in the world of the game ('avatar') and by means of this has to perform various tasks. In its basic form, this can occur solely via written text: The user types in certain commands ("go left" - "take item") and the program outputs the consequence of the order just typed ("now you stand in front of an old wooden door"). More advanced games involve realistic graphics, the player can see the world through the eyes of his avatar and decides which move he makes. Within this field, there are also a number of subgenres: "[...] Text only, Graphics, Character graphics, Drawn graphics, Bitmap Graphics, Interactive graphics, Moving character graphics, Point'n'Click, 3D, Text input, Sound, Music, Video Clips [...]" [2]

Moreover, according to SUTER [87, pp.31-32], there are at least five specific characteristics of interactive fiction:

[...] a) synchrones, bzw. unmittelbares, aktives Handeln der Rezipientin, das über Entscheidung, Aktion und Reaktion (Geschicklichkeit) geschieht; b) die Funktion von Rollenspielen für die Leserin, was eine Interaktion mit den andern Rezipienten in ihren Rollen notwendig macht; c) Relationen, die nicht immer vorhersehbar sind und sich durch die Interaktionen immer wieder verändern können; d) eine relative Auswahl bei der Anknüpfung und e) die Organisation in einem simulierten sozialisierten Umfeld als expansive Spiel- und Abenteuerwelt.

As a consequence I propose that - among other similarities - hyperfiction and the computer-games described share the characteristic of interactivity in a networked environment.

Net Art   As we shall see, this category is used to describe works found on the internet which combine multimedial elements to a higher degree. What has been termed 'hypermedia' above could also be subsumed under this category. Here, a significant number of innovative artists are being found on the web, constantly experimenting with new programs and technical developments. Parts of the artworks, moreover, are also transferred from the web to offline-installations which are then shown or even performed in museums. An important source of new works of this genre is *Rhizome*, a community

---

[2] http://www.lysator.liu.se/adventure/, quoted in [87, p.31]

which also serves as a platform for exchanging ideas and criticism. There are some rather 'exotic examples' of this branch of art: For instance, there are experiments and innovations such as a harmless computer-virus programmed only for the sake of enjoying its artistic qualities.

For this thesis, I have decided to use the term 'hypertext' in order to refer to the general concept of interlinked text-structures, and hypertext fiction, fictional hypertexts, and hyperfictions as synonyms to refer to the individual fictional works that are the focus of this analysis.

2.2. Definitions of Text

> [...] Die für Hypertext typische Verflechtung von Schrift, Bild, Ton und Video, die
> Redeweise vom nicht-linearen Lesen und Schreiben, der Wegfall physisch greifbarer
> Textgrenzen in einem sich stets verändernden "Dokuversum", der schnelle Rollen-
> tausch zwischenzug Produzenten und Rezipienten (die in diesem Medium Nutzer
> bzw. User heißen), rütteln an vertrauten Vorstellungen vom Text und führen
> schnell zu der Frage, ob derartige Gebilde überhaupt noch in den Zuständigkeitsbe-
> reich der Textlinguistik fallen, bzw. ob diese im Hinblick auf Hypertext einen
> neuen, erweiterten Textbegriff benötigt. [84, p.1.]

This statement made by STORRER - although primarily referring to text linguistics - is nevertheless quite revealing in view of the literary analysis of fictional texts on the internet. According to the author, the defining characteristics of hypertext - which will be referred to in detail in Chapter 3 - make it necessary to reach a clear understanding of 'text'. DAHLSTRÖM [35] argues:

> The conceptual confusion surrounding the term hypertext is, to a significant ex-
> tent, a result of the diverging definitions and uses of the text concept itself. If a
> discipline uses the term text to denote the signified, immaterial work created by
> an author, it consequently understands by hypertext the inter- and intratextual
> relations on the level of implied meaning. The equating of hypertextuality with
> the literary concept of *intertextuality* then makes a case. Where on the other
> hand text is used to denote signifiers, i.e. the manifested expression, hypertext as
> well will be a phenomenon at an expressional level of a document. Criteria such
> as *sequentiality* then become central. Where text implies an entity in reception
> theory and primarily describes the reader's interpretation and (re)creation of the
> graphic signs, then the concept of hypertext is one of *linearity* (the way the reader
> traverses the work). If, finally, text is defined from a narratological point of view,
> hypertext will foremost be a matter of story structure and plots.

This statement shows which different associations arise from the use of the concept of "text'" and from how many different angles this concept can be examined. It is therefore not surprising, as the author suggests, that it is hard to agree on a workable definition of hypertext. For the purpose this analysis, I suggest that it is important to discuss the individual works against the background of all the different points of view the author enumerates in the quotation above, i.e. the text as being produced by the writer, as manifested expression, as the readers' interpretation and finally as the outcome of the arrangement of story and discourse. Although this discussion is primarily concerned with applying suitable tools of narratological analysis to the body of primary hypertextual fiction, it is nevertheless necessary to refer briefly to the other viewpoints as well in order to position this analysis in the more general and comprehensive context of textual analysis.

In order to address this problem, I would firstly like to separate the 'hyper' from the 'text' and deal with the latter in some detail. For this purpose, I would like to discuss the paradigm suggested by DE BEAUGRANDE/DRESSLER [36]. According to the authors there are seven standards of textuality: 'cohesion', 'coherence', 'intentionality', 'acceptability', 'informativity', 'situationality', and 'intertextuality', which describe the communicative properties of texts in general. In the following paragraphs, I would like to give a rough outline of these seven standards and at the same time try to establish connections to hypertext.

Cohesion   The first standard, according to the authors, describes the way in which the individual components of a given text are connected grammatically. Using language in written as well as in oral communication is regulated by a series of rules which ensure the correct transmission of the respective items of information. An example of this are conjunctions within sentence constructions: A subclause related to the main-clause by the word "which" for instance indicates a relative clause and thus clearly establishes the connection to the subject of the main clause.

With regard to the analysis of fictional hypertexts, we can deduce that the standard of cohesion is especially suited to describe a text on an intrafragmental level: As will be shown in Chapter 5, every module of a text-network in most cases consists of a number of sentences, and the aspect of cohesion as well as its application to the text is comparable to traditional printed literature. On the interfragmental level, however, the establishment of cohesion is more problematic. Highly complex textual structures rely on high connectivity which would be hindered if one tried to bind them together by too rigid grammatical structures.

Coherence This standard is sometimes confused with 'cohesion', however, it is important to examine the different perspective this additional category allows for. While cohesion reflects the grammatical structuring of a text, coherence is concerned with the meaning, i.e. the semantic set-up of a given text. In other words, the single elements of a text need to be connected in a meaningful way so that their readings 'make sense'. In contrast to cohesion, the present concept quite fittingly describes the relationship between individual fragments on the interfragmental level. Even in a highly-fragmented text the author needs to make sure that the individual parts contribute to a coherent whole, i.e. all the fragments carry at least a small residue of coherence. In *The Unknown* for example, this overall-coherence is established by the motif of the narrative - in this case that of the travelogue.

Intentionality This feature describes to what extent a given text is suited to a communicative situation. As far as intentionality is concerned, I suggest that this standard can only be ascribed to fictional texts to a limited extent. The question "what did the author intend by using this special compositional feature" today is a very general question of interest only to the author-oriented subdisciplines of literary theories. However, the hypertext-author - compared to the writer of traditional printed literature - has got a number of additional tools[3] at his disposal in order to construct his work and gain the desired artistic effect. One of these is the use of links, which is discussed in detail in Chapter 3.2.4. The author can direct the individual readings and reading-paths of his text by establishing links and other navigational elements in a meaningful way.

---

[3]cf. Chapter 3.7 on authorship.

Acceptability Closely related to cohesion, coherence, and intentionality, but seen from the perspective of the recipient, the standard of 'acceptability' describes how successful the author is in constructing a text that is coherent and cohesive. Thus, the reader who is operating the text and browsing its individual fragments requires a degree of cohesion and coherence in order to continue the reading, diverge on different interesting paths and possibly engage in multiple reading sessions rather than losing a sense of coherence and "getting lost in hyperspace". Thus, especially in highly complex rhizomatic and maze-like hypertext-structures, it is vital for the author to provide the reader/user with a sense of where he is within the network, where the next links will lead him, and how the individual fragments contribute to a coherent work.

Informativity Yet another standard suggested by DE BEAUGRANDE/DRESSLER, which focuses on the reception-side of the communication-model, is the text's potential to present information that the reader has not received before, in other words, the text's informativity. This standard, however, provides more insights when seen in the context of nonfictional texts which supply the facts the reader is looking for. Concerning hypertext, this standard is especially interesting with regard to the way in which the individual textual fragments of the hypertext are arranged next to each other: If the author constructs a work of hyperfiction in such a way that some fragments are repeated over and over again, the informativity of these fragments amounts to zero.

Situationality Another standard the authors identify is that of situationality, i.e. the necessity to equip a given text with contextual information in order for it to 'make sense'. Again, the very structure of hypertexts provides a good experimenting ground for the application of this definition. An individual fragment of a hypertext is very rarely able to create meaning on its own, especially if it is rather short as in *My Boyfriend Came Back from the War* [12], where these fragments often take the form of single words. Only when seen in the context of the surrounding fragments does the single module actually contribute to a coherent reading. In the latter case, the individual lexias are arranged next to each other on screen, however, this is not always necessary. In *The Unknown* [9], the textual fragments are longer and for this reason they cannot appear simultaneously. Since all fragments are semantically connected, the overall context is always clear and thus the standard of situationality is fulfilled.

Intertextuality Especially the concept of 'intertextuality' will be looked at in more detail in Chapter 3.5 since it is a central characteristic of hypertexts. For DE BEAU-GRANDE/DRESSLER, a given text needs to be connected in an intertextual way to another one in order for this last standard of textuality to be fulfilled. As will be shown, hypertexts have got a very high affinity towards intertextuality, because no other textsort offers so many possibilities to establish links and connections.

In this chapter we have discussed how DE BEAUGRANDE/DRESSLER establish their conceptualisations of 'text'. Furthermore, it has become evident how all of these aforementioned categories can be applied to hypertexts in quite a successful way. As a summarising statement, then, I would like to quote STORRER [84, p.14]:

> Es gilt vielmehr, die neuen Textarten und Kommunikationsformen im Internet in Beziehung zu setzen mit Textarten und Kommunikationsformen, die bereits im Rahmen der Textlinguistik, der interdisziplinären Textverstehens- und Textproduktionsforschung oder der Gesprächsanalyse untersucht worden sind. Terminologische Differenzierungen sollten dann vor allem dem Zweck dienen, die Gemeinsamkeiten und Unterschiede zwischenzug "alten" und neuen Medien bezüglich Struktur, kommunikativer Function und kognitiver Verarbeitung möglichst gut greifbar zu machen.

2.3. 'Konzeptionelle Hypertextualität'

Having established a workable definition of text, it is now important to ask what makes the texts we are talking about 'hyper'.

Hypertext was not invented by the developers of elaborate interlinked computer software or the creators of the internet. Rather, the idea of links, which - as we will see later on - are the pivotal elements of hypertexts, can be found in printed literature as well. A modern encyclopedia, for instance, has a significant number of individual, self-contained texts which can be read in random order. Moreover, they are interlinked by what is referred to as cross-references and thus, according to NELSON's definition, the main requirements of hypertexts are met. By means of special markers, such as different letter-types, font-colours, or graphical items, links are established between different entries in the encyclopedia. It is then possible to refer to the respective item, which can even be in a different volume, and thus find one's way through the network of entries. Of course, in the example just quoted, there is much effort involved: Looking up different cross-references can indeed be time-consuming. However, qualitatively the act of browsing a network of texts basically remains the same. The user finds indicators of links and has to follow the pathway of information himself.

Using the electronic counterpart, for example the CD-ROM version of the same reference work, one would simply click on a cross-reference and be able to read the new entry within milliseconds. The cross-reference here works as a sort of transporter, i.e. the user is 'physically' moved to another location. In the electronic medium, this would be called a link. Although in the latter case, the retrieval of information is accelerated and enhanced by the new electronic medium, the organising principle behind it stays the same and is no innovation in itself. Hence, the question has to be raised, whether hypertext is or constitutes a new sort of text which needs its own descriptive tools?

A possible answer is provided by the manner in which Frauke INTEMANN deals with the subject. She introduces the term 'konzeptionelle Hypertextualität' (conceptional hypertextuality'), by means of which she establishes the crucial differentiation between the abstract characteristics of what we refer to as hypertext, and the medium which is used to present the respective work. This is reflected by SHILLINGSBURG, who is quoted by DAHLSTRÖM [35]:

2. Definitions and Categories

[I]t is possible for the same text to be stored in a set of alphabetical signs, a set of braille signs, a set of electronic signals on a computer tape, and a set of magnetic impulses on a tape recorder. Therefore, it is not accurate to say that the text and the signs or the storage medium are the same. If the text is stored accurately on a second storage medium, the text remains the same though the signs for it are different. Each accurate copy contains the same text; inaccurate or variant copies contain new texts [...]

In other words, hypertext as a concept is independent of the medium it is presented in: the main idea is the establishment of a network of text-fragments interconnected by links, in the sense NELSON had originally intended it.

As regards the actual realisations of hypertext, she also alludes to the so-called 'Affinitätsprinzip' introduced by KOCH/OESTEREICHER: Generally speaking, the model concedes that a work bearing the characteristics of 'konzeptionelle Hypertextualität', e.g. a work of hyperfiction, could also be presented in a non-digital form. INTEMANN [46, p.82] gives the following example:

Will man einen Hypertext in einen Zettelkasten überführen, dürfen die Links nicht fehlen. Alle verbundenen Datei-Zettel müssten mit einem Bindfaden auch physikalisch verbunden sein. Das wäre zwar unpraktisch, aber es wäre ein analoger Hypertext.

However, the production as well as the reception of such an analogue work would involve effort to the point of ridiculousness because readers would presumably spend more time physically accessing the respective file-slips than following the discourse. Thus, the model suggests that hypertexts have a higher *affinity* to the electronic medium. Here, they can be presented in a manner which makes producing and receiving them an actual aesthetic pleasure. Following the same logic, a long novel containing no links at all can also be published in an electronic environment. However, the fact that this computerised medium does not improve the reception of such a novel but rather decreases the pleasure of reading because of the less comfortable physical act, characterises this text-form to have a high affinity to the printed medium.

In summary, therefore, I suggest that there are two conceptionalisations of hypertext: on the one hand, there is the commonly assumed notion that hypertext is a text-sort mainly characerised by interlinking and its occurrence in an electronic environment. On the other hand, a more precise description of hypertext separates the concept from the electronic medium, which is what INTEMANN alludes to when she talks about 'konzeptionelle Hypertextualität'.

The 'real' hypertexts this dissertation is concerned with are all presented on the internet, and thus, as a literary phenomenon, they are inseparably connected to the medium they are transmitted in. Therefore, I will try to be careful not too "over-theorise" the actual texts, and point to the important dimensions that are added to the artistic value of the respective works by the technology that is used by the author. Or, to quote AARSETH [17, p.58]:

> [...] the electronic text, for all its hype and naivete, is still a text. If we accept this claim, then it seems clear that textuality cannot be defined in terms of location, anatomy, or temporality. What is the difference, in terms of script, between Don Quixote on paper and Don Quixote on a screen? I believe they are the same, although I "know" that the ink-cellulose relationship promotes and impedes different rituals of use than does the electron-phosphor relationship.

2.4. Genres

Defining genres may not initially seem particularly problematic but [...] it is a
theoretical minefield. [29]

In literary studies, according to WENZEL [90], the term 'Gattung' ('genre') is generally used in two different ways. Firstly, genre is used to describe one of the three major
literary categories, i.e. poetry, drama, and narrative. Secondly, it refers to the various text-types within these categories, such as tragedy, history, sonnet, limerick, gothic
novel or detective novel. Despite the numerous - and rather unsuccessful - attempts
to subdivide literature as a zoologist or a botanist would do with animals and plants
respectively, it is now recognised that "[...] weder im Gesamtfeld der literar. Texte
noch innerhalb der drei traditionellen Großbereiche klare Hierarchien über- und unter-
geordneter Kategorien auszumachen sind." WENZEL argues that genres are rather to
be understood as open and flexible systems, "[...] deren Charakter nur durch ein Bündel
von unterschiedlichen formalen, strukturellen und thematischen Kriterien beschrieben
werden kann." The awareness and the ability from the side of the reader to successfully
apply a generic label to a given text, however, varies to a considerable extent. Against
this background, CHANDLER [29] argues:

> Like most of our everyday knowledge, genre knowledge is typically tacit and would
> be difficult for most readers to articulate as any kind of detailed or coherent
> framework. Clearly one needs to encounter sufficient examples of a genre in order
> to recognise shared features as being characteristic of it.

The area of literary studies which concerns itself with establishing typologies and
developing the respective models is genre-theory ('Gattungstheorie'). In this context,
WENZEL describes how throughout history scholars have tried to approach the problem of finding universally valid models for the categorisation of literary texts, such as
for instance the concept of "Familienähnlichkeit" developed by Austrian philosopher
WITTGENSTEIN.[4] This approach, however, is often critised because it has been argued

---

[4] "[WITTGENSTEIN] meinte, es ließen sich keine allgemeinen Merkmale für alle Sprachen, Spiele und

that, depending from which point of view one takes, a text can resemble virtually any other.

With regard to the subject of research, I would like to highlight two examples of genres the characteristics of which could also be partly applied to hypertexts.

The Very Short Story   Fictional hypertexts have inherited some important characteristics from two genres of traditional printed literature, namely the very short story and comics, which I will briefly discuss here. I suggest that rather than seeing the analysis of hypertexts as an isolated entity, it makes more sense to discuss them against the background of the texts they have evolved from.

It can undoubtedly be argued that the whole range of analytical tools provided by narratology is not entirely suited for the analysis of hypertexts. For example, considerations such as elaborate characters and a complex plot-structure will not be particularly helpful, simply because the organising principle of hypertexts does not provide for these aspects. Similarly, the internal structure of the so-called 'short short story' or 'very short story' is marked by its brevity rather than elaborate development of characters. Concerning the actual writing of this kind of narratives, it has been argued that the text-production actually resembles writing poetry more than producing prose. STANZEL [83, pp.22-23] discusses this:

> [M]odern (Short) Short Story writers make demands on their readers which are
> closer to those of poets than to those of novelists. Reading a novel presents the
> reader mainly with the task of organizing in his memory long sequential patterns.
> Reading (short) short stories approaches the reading of poetry in shifting the

---

Sprachspiele herausstellen. Einige Spiele hätten zwar mit gewissen anderen gemeinsame Merkmale, aber mit wiederum anderen überhaupt keine. Und das zeige, daß "familienähnliche" Begriffe keine "universalen", d.h. für alle Einzelbeispiele gemeinsam zutreffenden Merkmale enthielten [...] An die Stelle identischer Merkmale setzte WITTGENSTEIN für die Begriffsbildung daher ähnliche Merkmale." [43, p.1]

attention to spatial, configurational patterns of textual organization, the single word or phrase, the line or sentence, to their symbolic or metaphorical rather than their referential meaning.

The last sentence of this quotation especially fits into our context, although it is doubtful that the scholar had these texts in mind originally. When he refers to "spatial, configurational patterns of textual organization", this could also be applied to the internal organisation of fictional hypertexts and the very concept of hypertext itself. In such an interlinked text, the individual textual fragments are arranged in (cyber-)space, which makes these texts 'hyper'. Thus, even from a very basic look at the defining characteristics of the very short story, it becomes evident how - with regard to genres - hypertexts have inherited characteristics of printed literature.

Comics A second genre I would like to sketch is that of comics, which are defined by MCCLOUD [60, p.9] as

Juxtaposed pictorial and other images in *deliberate sequence*, intended to convey information and/or produce an aesthetic response in the reader. *(my emphasis)*

The genre of comics, sometimes also referred to as cartoons or graphic novels, resembles hypertext in a number of ways. Firstly, like hypertext, it is an art-form that has not been fully accepted as such by academia. In fact, comics are still supposed to be only suited for children and teenagers, and as a genre unfit to transport a "deeper" meaning. Furthermore, the basic idea of comics relies on the combination of written text ('ballons') and graphics ('icons') in the so-called panels, i.e. the individual frames in which the plot takes place.

From these considerations it also follows that a reasonable analysis of hypertexts can only be performed by looking at the interaction and the mutual influence of written text and graphical items. Although it seems tempting to separate the two and talk about the language of comics and the text in the balloons, the full artistic effect which is intended by the writer is only truly transmitted by both their mutual and interdependent effects.

Likewise, we cannot neglect the interaction between all different layers of information in hypertexts. Even some structural characteristics are shared by these two genres in question: as Scott MCCLOUD [60, p.81] argues, works from Eastern culture, especially from Japan, tend to be of a more labyrinthine structure, rather than the European and American ones which are usually much more goal-oriented.

The concept of the panel in a comic can be compared to the screen in a piece of hyperfiction. In both respects, what the reader sees is contained within one separated space, and in both respects it is interesting to assess what can be seen and what is excluded. MCCLOUD argues that comics produced for readers in Western countries are usually read from left to right and from top to bottom, so the reading of the individual panels pretty much resembles the reading of a novel. However, as he convincingly argues, this is not always the case, and he gives examples of comics the artists of which uses this expectation to mislead the reader. Furthermore, he makes an interesting statement about sequentiality which could be seen as referring to hypertexts [60, p.106]:

> Comics readers are also conditioned by other media and the ' *real time* ' of everyday
> life to expect a very *linear progression*. Just a *straight line* from *point a* to *point*
> *b*. But is that *necessary*? For *now*, these questions are the territory of *games* and
> *strange little experiments*. But *viewer participation* is on the verge of becoming an
> *enormous issue* in *other media*.

As is often the case, there are no clear-cut subdivisions between genres, rather, we often witness a certain amount of overlap between them. Moreover, this overlap occurs not only with regard to form and structure, but also in connection with content: we can imagine a science-fiction story which, being based on a far-away planet, has traces of the Western-genre when the action takes place in a rural environment and its main protagonists are cowboy-like men. In this case, critics use the term 'hybrid genres' in order to account for these "borderline-texts". Although, following ERNST, the term is applicable every time the limits of a given genre are being crossed or expanded, it is mostly used in the context of the contemporary novel. Here, she especially emphasises the cases where there is a mixture between facts, i.e. nonfiction, and fiction in one and the same work:

> Dies ist z.B. der Fall, wenn authentisches Material mit Mitteln fiktionalen Erzählens
> strukturiert wird oder aber der Roman selbstreflexiv auf den Prozeß des Schreibens
> und damit auf seinen Konstruktcharakter verweist (Metafiktion).[39, p.220]

Stressing the metafictional character of a work, one is immediately reminded of the structure of hypertexts and the way they contain self-reflexive elements as well. Even more so, most hypertext authors deliver a thorough discussion of hypertexts which is integrated into the primary work, a good example of which is *The Unknown* (Cf. Chapter 6.2).

I suggest that with no other text-types can we witness metafictionality more than with regard to hypertexts. And since these works also cross existing borders of genres as has been suggested above, it seems justified to say that we can talk about hybrid genres in connection with hypertexts.

2.4.1. Genre Expectations

Another interesting aspect of the field of genre theory is the way in which readings of texts vary depending on the genre expectations we have. If we regard a genre as a kind of framework in which the interaction between producer and receiver, i.e. between author and reader occurs, then the shape and the set-up of the genre influence the way in which information is shared between the two. For example, it would be an interesting question to ask whether any given audience see a film differently - or even withdraw themselves entirely - when it is announced to them which genre it belongs to ('Western') or when this information is kept from them. In this respect, the concept of genre can be used to influence reader response to a certain extent, i.e. it can be instrumentalised.

> Contextual information influences both the process and the products of text com-
> prehension. A number of studies have demonstrated the influence of prior know-
> ledge in text comprehension [...][98, p.920]

In a series of experiments, undergraduate students were asked to read several short texts, which were extracts from both newspapers as well as from two novels. According to ZWAAN, prior to these experiments, it has been established that these extracts could "[...] pass as both literary and news stories [...]" [98, p.923]. Interestingly, depending on whether the subjects were told that a respective excerpt was either a news item or a piece from a novel, the readings varied.

These expectations can also be found with regard to hypertexts. When the reader/user accesses a specific text, he immediately develops a set of specific expectations simply because he uses the electronic medium and thus modifies his reading-behaviour. Having started to interact with the piece of programmed literature, the user will expect for instance navigational buttons, and underlined links. Arguably, the largest amount of literary hypertexts on the internet follows the usual conventions of this genre, however, there are nevertheless some instances which consciously deconstruct the reader-expectation and use navigational elements in new ways. A good example here is *IN MEMORY WE TRUST?* [6], which actually parodies an internet-page and thus misleads the expectations the readers/users have when trying to access tourist information on Verona.

2.4.2. Hypertext as a New Genre?

Regarding family-likeness, these texts share the characteristic of the electronic platform, be it the internet or any other mediator of digital information. Here, the user immediately modifies his reading behaviour: when switching on the computer and opening up the internet-browser, he knows how to use the conventions of this medium and employs various navigational strategies in order to retrieve the desired information or enjoy a fictional text that is based on these strategies. I suggest that this behaviour fits into the framework of genre expectations outlined above.

Finally, I suggest that also accounting for the metafictional character of most of the works we are going to discuss in this presentation, hypertexts can be called a "hybrid

2. Definitions and Categories

genre". Although it could be argued that each work of hyperfiction can also be attributed to the more general and already prevailing genres, we can imagine a science-fiction hypertext, a detective story hypertext or a Western hypertext. Following this line of argument, hypertexts would then only be electronic extensions of the genres established in print long before. While this is at least partly true with regard to the motifs and contents of the narratives, in my opinion it neglects the integrative potential of the electronic medium too much and therefore offers only a limited insight into these new texts.

> Die erkennbaren Entwicklungstendenzen von einfachen zu komplexen Formen, in diesem Fall vom elektronischen Text zu Text und Bild, zum Bild und weiter zum bewegten Bild und zu simulierten Umgebungen, bzw. von statischen Lesetexten zu interaktiven 'Multi-User-Welten', sind ein wichtiges Indiz für den Weg in Richtung einer neuen multimedialen Erzählform. Diese fliessenden Entwicklungen und Überschreitungen machen es nicht zuletzt immer schwieriger, klassische ästhetische Grenzen zu ziehen. [87, p.21]

As has been alluded to before, the field of hyperfiction is everything but homogenous. There is in fact a continuum between works involving multi-layered graphics, video and audio-information to a large extent, such as interactive computer-games or so-called web art on the one hand, and purely text-based works on the other. Likewise, there is a variety of categories that could be used as the basis for a generical subdivision. It is also interesting to find out how we can determine what characteristics a new genre usually exhibits. ZIEGFELD [96, p.359] argues in the following way:

> To determine whether this is a new form, I will compare interactive fiction with traditional literary elements, examine its technological devices, and then finally play it off against traditional literary genres and non-literary forms. An initial concern involves the larger question of how different a literary product must be if we are to designate it as "new". Essentially, the matter depends on (1) proportion of alteration from traditional to new forms and on (2) whether there are unique devices the new form introduces.

38

ZIEGFELD then compiles a list of criteria which in his opinion mark a new genre:

- Requires new production techniques

- Requires new aesthetic criteria to evaluate it

- Requires training for the user to know how to evaluate the product

- Leads to unique experiences

- Prompts genuinely new questions about the nature of the literary discipline

With regard to hypertexts, we can positively apply each of these prerequisites. Since the author needs to familiarise himself with certain programming languages and/or authoring software, the production of hypertext fiction involves new production techniques. As far as the new aesthetic criteria are concerned, as we will see in the course of this analysis, an interplay of existing genres and modes of presentation form the analytical toolbox for the evaluation and discussion of hypertext. On the side of the reader, some basic knowledge is required in order to be able to use the various tools offered by the computer-system and the internet-browser. If mastered, the reading of a work of hyperfiction can indeed be said to be a unique experience because of the combination of different types of media as well as the fact that one has to construct his own personal reading step by step through the network. In other words, hypertexts (and the overall-phenomenon) can quite justifiably be called a new genre.

2.4.3. Related Electronic Texts

For the sake of providing an overall-picture of the actual state of publications on the internet and to delineate its borders, I will briefly discuss so-called eBooks and print-on-demand-texts.

2.4.3.1. eBooks

The individual works of this kind do not need the networked environment in order to work. Rather, they are 1:1-adaptations of print-texts, which are distributed over the internet.

Project Gutenberg The most famous project containing texts that are transformed from the physical medium to the electronic one is the so-called *Project Gutenberg (PG)* [13]. Here, on a purely voluntary basis, members transform printed texts into electronic ones by retyping them or scanning them and using a text-recognition software - the texts are 'digitised' during this process. As for the aims of this project, we can read on the homepage:

> The premise on which Michael Hart based Project Gutenberg was: anything that
> can be entered into a computer can be reproduced indefinitely ... what Michael
> termed "Replicator Technology". The concept of Replicator Technology is simple;
> once a book or any other item (including pictures, sounds, and even 3-D items can
> be stored in a computer), then any number of copies can and will be available.
> Everyone in the world, or even not in this world (given satellite transmission) can
> have a copy of a book that has been entered into a computer.[5]

Evidently, the project is given the name of the inventor of movable-type mechanical printing: around the middle of the 15th century, Johann GUTENBERG invented a method of producing copies from a book faster and cheaper than was possible at the time when important works were manually copied by monks in cloisters. Thus, because of this technology, books became available to the masses. *Project Gutenberg*, which was

---

[5]`http://www.gutenberg.org/about/history`, accessed 25.04.05

started about 500 years later takes this idea a step further and focuses on the even
cheaper production of "books", targeting an even larger group of people around the
world. Copyrights for works of playwrights and authors like SHAKESPEARE and DICK-
ENS elapse after 70 years of the authors' death, and so it is now legal for individuals to
use these works and republish them on respective websites. Starting as early as 1971, at
a time when computers were still very expensive and accessible only to universities and
big companies, its founder Michael Hart typed in the first text of this massive online
library, which was the *Declaration of Independence.*

More than thirty years later, the library has had its 10,000th work - the *Magna Carta*
- added to the catalogue in December 2003. All works are available free of charge and
searchable by the users of one of the many pages that host the *PG* websites. Interested
readers can choose the work they are looking for and download the books in an electronic
format[6] which is readable on almost every computer-system in the world. These texts
can either be read directly on the screen or printed out on paper and read like a normal
book. Moreover, in recent times other types of media have been added to the database,
such as digitised music and free music-scores.[7]

---

[6]'Plain Vanilla ASCII' meaning the low set of the American Standard Code for Information Inter-
change.

[7]cf. `http://www.ibiblio.org/gutenberg/music/`. There are two other independent organisations,
which use the *Project Gutenberg* trademark by permission; these are the German and the Australian
PG sites. The German site `http://gutenberg.spiegel.de/` is a subsection of the "Kultur"-section
of *Spiegel Online*. As can be read there, it started in 1994, and to date (26.04.2005) there are about
420,000 pages of German text available to readers on the internet. Like its American counterpart,
the archive is fully searchable, texts can be found either via selecting an author, a title or a genre.
An internet company collects the works, reformats them into HTML and distributes them freely
on the web. The *Project Gutenberg of Australia* (`http://gutenberg.net.au/`) delivers free texts
according to Australian copyright specifications. Besides other works, it contains "The Project
Gutenberg Library of Australiana - Australian writers, works about Australia and works which
may be of interest to Australians" and lays emphasis on images and textual documents about the
settlement of the continent.

2. Definitions and Categories

Commercial eBooks In addition to hard- and softcovers, a number of publishing houses distribute their fiction via the internet, in the form of pdf-files for example. These files can then be printed out or read on the computer or handheld devices using special software. As with *Project Gutenberg*, these files are distributed via the internet, however, they are not free of charge. On the contrary, software companies such as MICROSOFT constantly develop new technologies like *DRM (Digital Rights Management)* to ensure that these works cannot be copied endlessly, and be sold like standard hard- or softcover books. Another contrast to *PG* is the fact that these books are being type-set in a professional manner, and they include graphics and images. The ideal way of accessing this type of book is by means of an electronic device called *eBook-reader*, which usually has the form and the size of a regular book, but includes a small computer monitor so that the works can be read electronically.

'Library of Amazonia' A similar way of providing internet users with online texts is pursued by the company *amazon.com*. In an attempt to attract the attention of potential customers, the company offers free excerpts of the books in question. The technology, which was given the name "Search inside the book", according to the company, offers better search results: "Now instead of just displaying books whose title, author, or publisher-provided keywords match your search terms, your search results will surface titles based on every word inside the book."[8] Reporting his experience with this new database and also this new type of knowledge, Gary WOLF [94] remarks:

> Amazon's new archive is more densely populated than the early Web was, but it's still far from complete. With its 120,000 titles, the archive has about as many books as a big brick-and-mortar store. Still, this is plenty to create a familiar sensation of vertigo as an expansive new territory suddenly opens up [...]

In order to create this database, printed works had to be digitised again, similar to procedure of the *Project Gutenberg*. However, here the effort has been much greater, the company has scanned printed books on an industrial scale.

---

[8]http://www.amazon.com/exec/obidos/tg/browse/-/10197021, accessed 25.04.05

As with *Project Gutenberg*, in terms of literary analysis of texts there are no new insights to be expected from these developments since the texts remain the same, only their distribution changes. However, the sociological aspects of these new technologies should not be neglected.

2.4.3.2. Print-on-Demand Texts

This category includes texts which first existed in an electronic environment and then have been turned into their physical (printed) form, which can be seen as the reversal of the production of eBooks. Nowadays everything that is intended to be published is initially conceived on a computer system - like the text of this presentation. Once the electronic form is established, it is then fairly easy to transform this text into a physical form. It can be printed out on a standard computer-printer, or used as a template for a printing press.

Apart from the everyday occurrences of this mode of publication, there is also one important project I would like to draw attention to. When the Government of the United States planned the pre-emptive military strike against Iraq in the first months of 2003, American poet Sam HAMILL was invited by Laura BUSH to a White House symposium on poetry. He asked a couple of fellow poets to send him poems "[...] speaking 'for the conscience of our country' in opposition to George BUSH's plans for a 'Shock and Awe' attack on Baghdad that would result in about 3,000 missiles hitting the city in the first two days of war. "[10, p.xvii] During the next month, about 11,000 poets submitted their poems to the website of *Poets Against the War*[9], making it an impressive voice against the plans of the government. When Laura BUSH learned about these plans, the symposium was cancelled, however, the poems left an impression":

> On March 5, in the company of fellow writers W.S. Merwin, Terry Tempest
> Williams, and Emily Warn, along with Poets Against The War board member
> Peter Lewis, I presented to Ohio Congresswoman Marcy Kaptur an electronic
> manuscript containing 13,000 poems by nearly 11,000 poets. It took a ream of

---

[9]`http://www.poetsagainstthewar.org`, accessed 25.04.05

paper to print just the names of contributors in three columns of small type. [10, p.xix]

The project is still active today, and successively poems are added to the database. What is interesting in this respect is the fact that a selection of these texts have been published as a printed book. This anthology represents an interesting transfer from electronic to printed form, being also a good example of the cross-mediality of the genre. The reasons for publication are manifold. As many theorists on the subject suggest, a book made of paper is still the preferred way of receiving literature for most people, so the preference has mostly haptical reasons.

2.4.3.3. CD-ROM Hypertext

Although it is not the main-subject of this presentation, a couple of remarks need to be made with regard to hypertext distributed exclusively via CD-ROMs like those by American publisher EASTGATE. As has been alluded to in the introduction, the only hypertexts which have been more thoroughly been analysed were the ones published on this medium.

This alternative mode of distribution has several implications. Since these texts are sold on a commercial basis, the mode of production resembles more the 'established' practice of print-literature, with authors being able to sell their works to a publishing house. So, rather than treating the production of hyperfiction as a hobby or experimenting ground, authors like Michael JOYCE, Shelley JACKSON and Stuart MOULTHROP write hyperfiction professionally. The works are characteristically closer to their printed counterparts because the text-borders are clearly defined: although - once installed on one's home computer - various reading-paths can be saved and added to the main text, the text as it is stored on the medium is unchangeable in itself. Like a printed work, the work of hyperfiction on CD-ROM consists of a fixed and unchangeable number of textual fragments. Thus, this mode of production implies a stability that cannot be found to such an extent on the internet. With regard to the latter, as has been mentioned elsewhere, the fragments are of an ephemeral character, constantly threatened by either deliberate or accidental deletion from the respective online-server it is stored on.

2.4.3.4. Nonfiction

An area that is frequently referred to and analysed is the area of nonfictional hypertexts, especially virtual learning environments. Current research attempts to identify whether the node-structure of hypertext-networks can be used to teach certain subjects more successfully than by using printed 'linear' literature. For this reason, there have been a range of empirical studies, some of which have appeared in *Lesesozialisation in der Mediengesellschaft* [45]. A common assumption is that the use of hypertexts would automatically imply better understanding and learning of facts, however, CHRISTMANN et.al. [33, p.179] argue:

> Vielmehr ist davon auszugehen, daß Hypertexte und lineare Texte unterschiedliche Arten der Informationsdarbietung darstellen, die für verschiedene Zielsetzungen unterschiedlich gut geeignet sind. Entsprechend kommt es darauf an, zu prüfen, in welchem Ausmaß Rezipienten/innen in der Lage sind, die je spezifischen Verarbeitungsanforderungen zu erfüllen. Dabei soll in systematischer Weise auf die am linearen Buchmedium herausgearbeiteten Verarbeitungsstrukturen zurückgegriffen werden, insbesondere auf die Forschung zu Lernstrategien, Metakognition, Textverständnis/-verständlichkeit; und zwar vor allem zur Klärung der Frage, welche Verarbeitungskompetenzen auf Hypertexte übertragbar sind und welche nicht, wobei im zweiten Fall neue Lösungsperspektiven erarbeitet werden müssen.

Hence, what has been taken for granted by the early hypertheorists cannot be entirely taken at face value. Intuitively, it might seem self-evident that by presenting information in a fragmented and networked way, it is easier to access because of a more associative approach to information retrieval. However, it is not automatically the case - at least in view of existing empirical analyses - that this information is processed any better or faster by the respective recipient.

The first hypertexts on the internet were non-fictional, educational information-networks. George LANDOW, hypertext theorist (and enthusiast) of the late 1980s, has created a number of so-called "webs", which were the results of a joint effort of students of BROWN

UNIVERSITY to a considerable extent. In this vein, especially the *Victorian Web*[10] springs to mind, with its sheer endless amount of textual fragments and interlinking. Although from a modern perspective this website almost appears to be prehistoric and very user-unfriendly, it nevertheless seems to have paved the way for other generations of multi-medial hypertext structures found on the internet today.

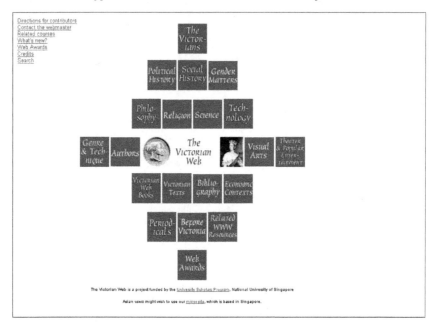

Figure 2.1.

"The Victorian Web"

Here, the user is invited to access one of the various subjects and themes such as 'Philosophy', 'Science', 'Technology' and so on by clicking one of the square-shaped icons which lets him enter the text and browse all aspects of the Victorian Age. 'Philosophy' leads to a fragment containing a list of all the important contemporary philosophical considerations and their representatives. Here, the word 'Utilitarianism' leads to a fragment about the life and work of Jeremy BENTHAM which yet again contains links to his writing. In other words, the whole project is set up to work like a gigantic online-

---

[10]`http://www.victorianweb.org/`, accessed 25.04.05

encyclopedia, enabling readers to follow interesting parts very quickly rather than having to refer to the volumes of the printed version of this text.

Likewise, there are many more of these informational and non-fictional hypertexts on the internet, ranging from academic discussions supported by citations, audio- and video-supplements to personal homepages of regular people presenting their hobbies and their photographs.

Having thus completed our overview of hypertextual writing as it exists today, I would now like to elaborate on the structural characteristics of hyperfiction.

3. Characteristics of Hypertext

> Reading through a hypertext, one senses that just under the surface of the text
> on the screen is a vast reservoir of story waiting to be found. [34, p.9]

This chapter examines the various characteristics that are commonly associated with hypertexts. The most important issues will be discussed and prominent approaches will be tested for their plausibility. I have chosen to do so because there seems to be a considerable degree of vagueness concerning various concepts. As has been mentioned before, most of the traits of hypertext have been attributed to postmodern literary criticism:

> Pedantic postmodernism is the natural center of most hypertheory. Poststructuralism is the official doctrine: "Most poststructuralists write from within the twilight of a wished-for coming day; most writers of hypertext write of many of the same things from within the dawn," George P. Landow, prominent hypertheorist at Brown University, writes with excitement.
>
> [...]
>
> Derrida and de Man, Barthes and Baudrillard, Calvino and Cortazar, Pynchon and Borges; in hypertheory, the same postmodern Olympians are being quoted over and over again. [75, p.312]

What follows is a role-call of these 'Olympians' together with the most important concepts they have proposed:

> [T]heorists of electronic textuality have found parallels with the work of numerous French theorists: DERRIDA, FOUCAULT, LYOTARD, BAUDRILLARD, DELEUZE and

3. Characteristics of Hypertext

GUATTARI. The aspects of contemporary literary theory that find their fulfilment in hypertext hardly need explanation: The open text. Meaning as reconfigurable network. The slipperiness of the signifier and the deferral of meaning (symbolised by the system of links). Intertextuality. Reading as "exploding the text" and as endless activity. (You never know if you have seen all the lexemes, and travelled all the links of a hypertext.) Non-linearity. The death of the author. The empowerment of the reader[...][73]

Rather than elaborating on postmodern literary theory - this has been performed amply by hypertheorists in my opinion - I would like to discuss the features of hypertexts as they occur in secondary literature from different areas of literary studies.

On a more general level, DAHLSTRÖM [35] establishes a convincing subcategorisation of the features of all digital texts, which in his opinion are 'immateriality', 'binarity', and 'dynamics'. Then, on a more specialised level, namely discussing internet hypertexts in particular, he identifies 'kinetics', 'markup/text as hierarchy', 'fragmentisation', and 'hypertextuality'.

Immateriality, which is the first category the author proposes, refers to the most obvious characteristic of electronic texts, namely the way they exist only as binary data on a data-carrier such as a CD-ROM or a harddisk rather than a printed book. In other words, the textual manifestation of an electronic text is far less visible - and tangible for that matter - and needs an elaborate mechanism in order to be deciphered and consumed by the reader. In contrast, the printed book is a physical item that one can see and feel and that can be received "as is". Thus, in the latter case, the text is displayed and stored in the same medium. In the same vein, KEEP [51, p.170] suggests:

In a very real sense, there is no such "thing" as a hypertext, an object one can hold in the hands, a single, identifiable construct which would mirror the subject's own fragile sense of autonomy. Hypertexts exist *in potentia*, as a skittering of electronic impulses which take no determinate form until invoked by the computer's operating system.

With 'electronic impulses' the author refers to the basic elements of every digital file. Here, DAHLSTRÖM [35] coins another special term, binarity, which describes this phenomenon. He suggests that regardless of what form an electronic text has, i.e. a written text, a sound-file, a video-clip, or a graphical image, ultimately it consists of a succession of 1 and 0 digits. On the electro-physical and the optical-physical level, these digits are either stored on a hard-disk as either magnetic or non-magnetic spots, or on CD- or DVD-ROM as little bumps and holes on the surface of the medium. Through various programming-levels within the computer it is then possible to translate these sequences into a state that can be projected on a computer-screen and be read by the reader. Quite fittingly, the author talks about a digital *lingua franca* in this context.

Furthermore, DAHLSTRÖM identifies another way in which this immateriality has effects on the contents of the story itself: "[...] The obvious correlation between the length of a printed text and the spatial extension of its artefactual carrier (i.e., the book) simply ceases in the digital realm." In other words, since the text is no longer physically confined between two book-covers, it becomes harder to trace the actual borders of the electronic texts - most importantly, it becomes difficult to trace the ending for example. This will also be the focus in Chapter 3.6 on the relationship between open and closed texts.

Another characteristic that, according to the author, is brought about by the immaterial character of the texts in question is what he refers to as 'dynamics'. DAHLSTRÖM draws our attention to the fact that technically speaking, it is quite easy to migrate an electronic text to the printed medium, which is the case for instance when a text which has been written by means of a text-processor is printed out. Furthermore, this is also possible *vice-versa*: using a scanner and a text-recognition software it is possible to transfer a printed work into its electronic counterpart. As a result, the electronic text seems to be unstable and even 'liquid' since it can be cast into another physical form with little effort. However, as DAHLSTRÖM [35] reminds us, "[A]ll material text carriers crumble away by time, be it stone, wood, textiles, paper, woodpulp, plastic or silicon."

In a second line of argument, the author becomes more specific and describes what he refers to as 'webtexts' and their typical characteristics: Using a technical term from physics - "[...] the branch of mechanics concerned with the forces that cause motions of bodies [...]"[1] - the author describes webtexts as being 'kinetic': He argues that because of the speed with which new links can be followed, fragments can be opened, and the text-form can be changed, as discussed above, we can talk about the kinetic "forces" at play here. This is also true for the "[...] emendation, editing, refreshing, and instant republishing[...]" of these texts. As far as the act of publishing is concerned, the author suggests that another quite obvious feature of most hypertexts on the internet is the way in which they are internally organised and programmed in a mark-up language. As we will see in Chapter 4, the *Hypertext Mark-Up Language (HTML)* is used in order to format the text the reader sees on the screen. In other words, the author can specifically determine for every item that is eventually visible on the screen, where it is positioned, which font-size or -colour it should be shown in and so on. The effect is that when we are approaching hypertexts in order to analyse them, we are faced with two textual layers, namely the content- and the code layer, which will be discussed in more depth in Chapter 4.4.

The final characteristics DAHLSTRÖM explicitly refers to are 'fragmentisation' and 'hypertextuality'. I suggest that these two features represent the core of all further analytical discussion of hypertexts. The author argues that the texts on the internet are fragmented to a very high degree, be it within a fragment and its different textual layers or regarding the whole distribution of fragments within the textual space.

INTEMANN [46], in addition, broadly identifies the main characteristics of hypertext as being the 'elektronische Plattform' ('electronic platform'), 'Nicht-Linearität' ('non-linearity'), 'Hyperlinks' ('hyperlinks'), 'Unklarheit der Textgrenzen' ('unclarity of text-

---

[1] http://www.hyperdictionary.com/dictionary/kinetics, accessed 25.04.05

borders'), and 'Interaktivität' ('interactivity'). I shall now discuss these characteristics in the ensuing chapters.

3.1. Linearity

> [...] our view of text as an ordered succession of concepts is strongly reinforced by
> the constraints of the standard print medium: texts come to us on printed pages
> that we generally read in order, from the top down and from left to right. [31,
> p.110]

According to LIESTØL [57, p.103], "[N]onlinearity has generally been seen as one of the distinguishing hallmarks of hypertext [...]". A common conception is that in contrast to printed - and thus characteristically linear - literature, a reader of a hypertext is free to choose his path through the nonlinear network. However, as INTEMANN, LIESTØL, and STORRER remind us, since the concept has been used inflationarily in various contexts, it is necessary to have a closer look at its numerous implications.

For a hypertext, the underlying programming-structure of the work usually remains invisible to the reader. And although he gets a sense of having the choice between various strands of the plot in a tree-structured hypertext for instance, the actual reading process is typically linear. The human brain receives information organised on a temporal axis, and hence information can only be recognised and stored when delivered in sequentially ordered pieces. If one wrote down the text of even the most highly fragmented hypertext on paper, the outcome would resemble a printed text. INTEMANN refers to this when she argues:

> Auf dem Bildschirm des Lesers entsteht ein Text durch nacheinander rezipierte In-
> formationseinheiten, unabhängig von der Struktur des Systems. Das Konzept der
> Nicht-Linearität beschreibt also nicht den strukturellen Aufbau, die Architektur
> eines Hypertexts, sondern allein die Tatsache, dass der gesamte Text in Informa-
> tionseinheiten aufgespalten ist. [46, p.117]

In other words, although it is possible to encounter highly complex and interwoven structures in hyperfiction, the individual readings - although being more numerous because of the very structure of the text - are comparable to those of printed texts. In the same vein, LIESTØL [57, p.106] makes the necessary distinction between nonlinearity in 'time' and in 'space':

> Nonlinearity in time is imaginary; it is a fundamental contradiction of terms and necessarily impossible. *Time* is *linear*, at least the time that is required to read and write hypertexts. Reading and writing are linear phenomena: they are sequential and chronological, conditioned by the durative ordering of time, although their *positions* as stored *in space* may have a nonlinear organization.

In addition to the term nonlinearity, INTEMANN suggests the term 'zero-linearity': She argues that even in a highly fragmented work of hyperfiction there is still a small residue of linearity: the individual fragments are written in a sequential order themselves. In contrast, zero-linearity exists, when the text is atomised to individual words or even smaller linguistic entities, such as morphemes for example. This extreme fragmentation, however, is hardly able to transport any textual meaning and as a consequence is very rarely found on the internet at all, apart from word-art experiments.

In the same vein as INTEMANN's differentiation between hypertextuality as a concept and as a concrete manifestation, STORRER develops the binary opposition between what she terms 'konzeptionelle Linearität' ('conceptional linearity'), which she also refers to as 'Sequenziertheit', and 'mediale Linerarität' ('medial linearity'). She argues that there both are media which are inherently 'linear' and 'non-linear':

> *Lineare Medien* übermitteln Daten in einem fest vorgegebenen zeitlichen Nacheinander, das bei der Rezeption nicht oder nur schwer unterlaufen werden kann. Beispiele sind Tonkasetten [sic], Filmrollen oder Videokasetten [sic]. [...] Bei *nicht-linearen Medien* können die Daten in unterschiedlicher Abfolge rezipiert werden. In diesem Sinne ist auch das Buch ein nicht-lineares Medium. Zwar präsentiert es die Daten in räumlichen Nacheinander; der Rezipient hat jedoch die Möglichkeit, nur partiell und quer gegen diese Abfolge zu lesen. [84, p.19]:

The last example of the book, the death of which has been often proclaimed by early hypertext-theorists (and -enthusiasts), especially shows how different structural levels of this literary phenomenon are mixed and therefore misunderstood. The bound volume as such, in other words, is a medium that - like the individual textual fragments in a hypertext-system on the internet - is characteristically non-linear since one can refer to single pages, leaf through it randomly or skip certain passages. However, works that are mostly published using this medium are conceptionally linear, meaning that usually one reads a book from cover to cover, so that it might indeed *seem* as if a book was a linear medium. In order to develop the concept of 'konzeptionelle Linearität', STORRER [84, pp.20-21] makes the following subdivision:

In *monosequenzierten Texten* plant der Autos einen thematisch kontinuierlichen Leseweg, auf dem sich jedes Textsegment inhaltlich-thematisch auf der Grundlage der bereits rezipierten Textsegmente einordnen lässt [...] Beispiele für monosequen- zierte Textarten sind argumentative Texte (z.B. Urteilsbegründungen), erzählende Texte (z.B. Märchen und Novellen) und bestimmte Informationstexte (z.B. wis- senschaftliche Monographien und Fachartikel) [...]

Mehrfachsequenzierte Texte sind auf eine Lektüre von Anfang bis Ende nicht mehr ausgelegt. Statt dessen gibt es verschiedene Lesewege, aus denen sich die Rezipienten diejenigen auswählen, die ihrem Vorwissen und ihrem aktuellen In- formationsbedarf am besten entsprechen [...] Beispiele sind bestimmte Infor- mationstexte (z.B. Reiseführer, Computerhandbücher) und mehrfachadressierte Lehrbücher bzw. Monographien [...]

Bei *unsequenzierten Texten* wird auf Lesepfade gänzlich verzichtet. Die Textkon- stituenten sind durch thematische Verweise miteinander verknüpft und können ohne Risiko für das Verständnis in beliebiger Abfolge rezipiert werden [...] Beispiele für unsequenzierte Textsorten sind Wörterbücher und Lexika.

The issue of linearity is also closely connected to the organisation of the narrative elements within a specific text. There are a number of literary genres which rely very much on linear or sequential order. With regard to this, STORRER [84, p.18] pointedly asks:

3. Characteristics of Hypertext

> Wie soll es einem nicht-sequenzierten Krimi gelingen, einen Spannungsbogen auf-
> zubauen? Wie kann ein Witz funktionieren, bei dem es dem Rezipienten freisteht,
> die Pointe zuerst, mittendrin oder zuletzt zu lesen?

Indeed one can hardly imagine a detective story working in a hypertextual environment. A work belonging to this genre usually follows certain conventions, such as the
murder, the subsequent search for the murderer and the final solution. If one imagines
that it could be possible to find out who the murderer is by reading the respective lexia
in a work of hyperfiction, it is at least doubtful whether suspense can be created at all.

3.2. Links

> The use and placement of links is one of the vital ways in which the tacit assumptions and values of the designer/author are manifested in a hypertext - yet they are rarely considered as such. [27, p.105]

Both for hypertexts, as for the whole internet, the pivotal element is the interconnection between the fragments of information we refer to as 'links'. By using various markers to indicate the link, the authors of literary hypertexts as well as other informational internet-sites encourage the readers to click it and thus be transported immediately to the next fragment. The more links that are offered, the more the work turns into a maze-like structure; hence, the complexity and the resulting way of reception of a single work draws ultimately on the quality and the quantity of links, which is the reason why we should pay special attention to it.

Generally speaking, according to BURBULES, links directly influence the reception of texts not only by their way of constructing possible reading paths through the structure, but also by simply arranging fragments next to each other ("[...] how will a jump from a page on teenage drug-use statistics to a page on rock music affect how the rock music page is read?[...]" [27, p.105]). Also, referring to the analysis of links and interlinked structure, he suggests:

> The more that one is aware of *how* this is done, the more one can be aware *that* it was done and that it *could* have been done otherwise. This discloses the apparent 'naturalness' or invisibility of such designer/author choices, and grants the hyperreader the opportunity to stand outside them - to question, criticise, and imagine alternatives. Links are made, and they are made by specific individuals and groups according to their own assumptions, prejudices, and limitations. [27, pp.118-119]

According to STORRER [86, p.7], there are three different tasks that a link has to perform:

Link-Kennzeichung "Die Rezipienten müssen erkennen können, welche auf dem Bildschirm sichtbaren Objekte als Links fungieren, d.h. die betreffenden Objekte müssen als Linkanzeiger erkennbar sein [...]"

Link-Explikation "Der Autos muss deutlich machen, was passiert, wenn ein Link aktiviert wird, d.h. er muss die Wahloptionen für den Nutzer semantisch und funktional transparent machen [...]"

Link-Positionierung "Der Autos muss die Links im Hypertext-Modul an der richtigen Stelle platzieren [...]"

3.2.1. Navigation

The most important devices in the process of reading a work of hyperfiction is the array of navigational tools the reader can use in order to master the text. As with most of the discussion of hypertexts, here we find yet another instance of how the primary texts are really regarded as spaces that can be traversed: together with the common image of "surfing", the internet is indeed compared to an 'ocean of information', and one needs to make sure to both incorporate and use the right "guides" in order not to shipwreck.

The effectiveness of navigation in a given piece of hypertext has been closely analysed with regard to creating electronic learning environments. And although empirical studies have been performed in the context of how successful students were in navigating a given non-fictional and educational hypertext, the topic of navigation is also quite important for the study of literary hypertexts. ROUET/LEVONEN [71, p.16] report how ill-configured structuring and accessing can lead to confusion and disorientation on the side of the reader:

> In a study by Foss [...] hypertext readers tended to "loop" in the hypertext, and to flip through pages instead of reading them carefully. Self-reports indicated that looping and flipping did not reflect deliberate strategies but resulted from a disorientation problem. Subjects reported difficulties in defining an optimal

reading order, and in locating themselves in the network.

Hence, the often witnessed 'lost-in-cyberspace' phenomenon is mainly based on the internal organisation of the respective hypertext. Authors can avoid this problem by arranging the navigational tools in an understandable way and thus facilitate the reception of their texts. On the other side of the act of communication, the reader needs to engage actively with the text because "[C]ompared to linear text, hypertext imposes a higher cognitive load on the reader: The reader must remember her location in the network, make decisions about where to go next, and keep track of pages previously visited." [71, p.17]

In what follows, I would like to examine some of the possible strategies authors can employ to construct tools for navigation. STORRER [85, pp.11] suggests the following strategies in order to avoid problems of reception:

Structure overviews "[...] support the user in developing a mental model of the size and the structure of the hyperdocument or site, thus compensating for the problem of 'informational shortsightedness' [...]". A good example here is the usage of so-called site-maps that could best be described as very detailed tables of contents, showing the individual fragments and their internal hierarchical organisation.

Global context cues "[...] emphasize the topical contribution of each single node to the global theme of the hyperdocument [...]". Here for instance, by using different markers like icons and colours the author of a hypertext marks the end of the original hypertext and the beginning of an external one, linked by these so-called external links.

Local context cues "[...] list the target nodes that are accessible from the currently visited node, and explain how they are semantically related [...]". In most modern browsers, the user is given a short information in the so-called status bar in the lower left corner of the monitor, as to where the link that is being touched will lead to. This also pops up immediately next to the link itself.

Since these tools are crucial for the creation of coherent readings, I would like to introduce these categories into our analytical toolkit in order to examine the corpus against the background of their internal navigational structure. As for the way in which the introduction of different navigational tools into a hypertext can be analysed from a cognitive perspective, I would like to refer readers to *Hypertext and Cognition* by ROUET/LEVONEN [71], which contains some very convincing empirical approaches.

3.2.2. Link vs. "Verweis"

Comparing electronic links to cross-references, STORRER [86, p.7] identifies several similarities and differences between the printed and the electronic medium:

> Gerade die unidirektionalen, textintegrierten, nicht-typisierten Links, wie sie für die HTML-basierte WWW-Technologie typisch sind, lassen sich recht zutreffend als computerisierte Verweise beschreiben: Prototypische Verweise sind erkenntlich an einem Verweisanzeiger [...] beim Verweissprung, und einer Spezifikation des Verweisziels, das allerdings vom Nutzer selbst identifiziert und aufgefunden werden muss. Links im WWW sind erkenntlich durch Linkanzeiger beim Linkursprung: die Aktivierung des Linkanzeigers per Mausklick lässt das Verweisziel am Monitor erscheinen, d.h., der Computer nimmt dem Nutzer die Verweisverfolgung ab [...]

Still, as she convincingly argues, there are two major differences between the two that also have to be kept in mind:

- "Da das Linkziel weder selbst erschlossen noch durch Hin- und Herblättern aufgefunden werden muss, erhöht sich die Wahrscheinlichkeit der Verweisverfolgung erheblich [...]"

- "Man kann sich gedruckte Nachschlagewerke ohne Verweise vorstellen, Hypertexts ohne Links sind undenkbar. Dies gilt besonders für navigatorische Links, die zu den jeweils zentralen Dreh- und Angelpunkten der zugehörigen Site führen [...]"

Hence, although there are parallels between the conventional cross-references and electronic links, it is compulsory to note the additional functions the latter can fulfill.

3.2.3. Link as Theme/Rheme-Relationship

> Hyperlinks sind im WWW oft durch anklickbare Wörter oder Phrasen realisiert,
> die das Thema definieren. Das Rhema kann in einem solchen Fall selbst einen
> komplexeren Text darstellen, von dem aus weitere Thema-Rhema-Verbindungen
> abzweigen. [46, p.96]

Furthermore, as a strategy for consistency- and coherence-building in hypertextual fiction, INTEMANN identifies the 'theme-rheme-relationship'. Usually, the 'theme' of a sentence can also be referred to as the topic, meaning the part of the sentence that is already known. In contrast, the 'rheme' - also called 'comment' - is the part of the text unit that conveys the new information. With regard to the characteristics of links as such, the marker inviting the user to click could be seen as the 'rheme' of the "old" lexia, and at the same time becomes the 'theme' of the "new" lexia that the user is being transported to.

3.2.4. Classification of Links

Following INTEMANN [46, p.110], it is possible to differentiate between three different types of links: 'intrahypertextual links', which are found within one fragment of a hypertext structure, 'interhypertextual links' connecting various fragments of one hypertext structure, and 'extrahypertextual links' linking one specific work or entity to other structures surrounding it. The first group is of only marginal importance for our further analysis because it is very rarely the case that we find a fragment in hypertextual fiction which is long enough for an intrahypertextual link to make sense. These links are more often found in non-fictional and purely informative internet-pages. By means of so-called 'anchors' which are programmed into the mark-up language which lies underneath the visible text, certain passages within a long fragment can be accessed more quickly and directly.

The most important group for the further study of hypertexts is the second one: 'interhypertextual links'. It can be argued that this type of interconnection between two fragments of a fixed structure is at the same time the constituting element of all hypertextual writing. Bearing in mind the initial conception of hypertext by NELSON, these interhypertexual links make browsing a hypertextual work possible in the first place.

Extrahypertextual links gain importance when viewed against the background of the concept of intertextuality: INTEMANN suggests that this group of links establishes interconnections between various individual works. However, as can be imagined, the existence of these links also undermines our understanding of fixed textual entities as such, because the more extrahypertextual links are being established between two independent works, the more the very border between them is blurred.

Apart from their structural occurrence, links can also be classified according to the poetic function they take in the context of the individual work. Interestingly, BURBULES [27, pp.110-117] undertakes the task of attributing various characteristics of commonly known tools of rhetorics to links. Although sometimes it seems as if the author does not specifically focus on links but rather on more general characteristics and norms of the internet, the following list of the examples he gives will provide some interesting categories for our analytical toolset.

3.2.4.1. Links as metaphor

> Web links can be read as metaphors when apparently unrelated textual points are associated: a link from a page listing Political Organisations to a page on the Catholic Church might puzzle, outrage, or be ignored - but considered as a metaphor it might make a reader think about politics and religion in a different way. [27, p.111]

A metaphor is defined by WHALLEY [92, p.490] as a "[...] condensed verbal relation in which an idea, image, or symbol may, by the presence of one or more other ideas, images, or symbols, be enhanced in vividness, complexity, or breadth of implication [...]" and I suggest that this is the most commonly and most well-known figure of speech that can be found in literature.

Metaphors consist of two parts: the 'tenor' and the 'vehicle'. If we take an example such as "life is a highway", 'life' would be called the tenor, i.e. the subject of the metaphor, and 'highway' the vehicle which is applied to the tenor. The metaphor in this example works because both vehicle and tenor share the same ground, i.e. both can be "long and winding". As regards metaphors, therefore, it is possible to find a parallel with the technical realisation of links. Usually, a link consists of a word or a graphical item clearly marked as the link-trigger, and the link-target which is the specific page the user is being lead to after having clicked the trigger. In this context, the trigger could be called tenor, and the resulting page the vehicle: both the underlined link-trigger and the target share a thematic ground which can be determined by the author of the hypertext. And although this relationship is usually fixed, it does not necessarily imply that the respective target-fragment only responds to one special trigger. On the contrary, it is often the case that a target-fragment can be accessed via several different triggers, resulting in varying readings of one and the same module. This is also what BURBULES refers to in the example quoted above.

3.2.4.2. Links as Metonymy

> A Web link, almost by definition can become metonymic, with repetition. Most
> users no longer have to be told that clicking on a pentagon-shaped icon will take
> them 'home', to the index or entry-page of a set of interlinked pages. [27, p.112]

In the context of links, we can also find that they perform a task similar to 'metonomy', which is defined as a "[...] figure [...] in which one word is substituted for another with which it stands in close relationship."[40, p.499] Here, in order to exemplify this, the author gives an example from *Romeo and Juliet* (3.1.163): "[...] he tilts/With piercing steel at bold Mercutio's breast." Hence, the steel refers to a dagger which is made of steel and is thus semantically connected to it. This relationship can also exist via the link-trigger and the target-fragment, for example when a website contains the word "leather" marked as link, which transports the reader/user to a site about football.

3.2.4.3. Links as Synecdoche

> In the context of Web links, this trope is particularly influential in identifying, or
> suggesting, relations of categorical inclusion: a list of 'Human Rights Violations'
> may include links to pages dealing with corporal punishment in schools, or vice
> versa. [27, p.112]

Quite similar to the trope of metonomy is synecdoche, which is sometimes referred to
as a specialised version of the former, in which a part stands for the whole ('pars-pro-
toto'). In this sense, a sail can stand for a ship for example. As BURBULES argues in
the statement cited above, usually this figure of speech can be seen as being related to
the way that single web-pages are situated within a more general context. The binary
opposition which we have established before, namely the one of link-trigger and target-
fragment, is also applicable in this context. The trigger denotes the 'pars' and leads
directly to the larger semantic framework in the target, the 'toto'. What is especially
interesting in the latter case is that by means of using links as synedoches, hierarchies
are established, because a target-frame could also be seen as a 'pars' for an even broader
context and so on.

3.2.4.4. Links as Hyperbole

> [E]ach collection, each archive, each search engine, tacitly implies a degree of
> comprehensiveness beyond its actual scope. For all its wealth and complexity, the
> Web comprises only a fraction of culture, society, and politics, worldwide [...] [27,
> p.113]

In this case, BURBULES seems to deviate from his line of argument a little bit since
with the trope of hyperbole he refers more to the characteristics of the internet itself
rather than focussing specifically on links and the relationship between trigger and target.
Naturally, all the hyperbolic exaggerations of the internet are embodied by links since
they are the combining element of the networked structure. Nevertheless I suggest that
with regard to the actual narrative function of links, the hyperbole is of no particular
relevance in our context.

3.2.4.5. Links as Antistatis

> Many Web links work this way: using a particular word or phrase as a pivot from
> one context to a very different one. Key-word search engines are based almost
> entirely on this principle. [27, p.113]

Antistatis is defined as the "[...] repetition of a word in a contrary sense. Often,
simply synonymous with antanaclasis."[2]. A good example for the latter is Benjamin
FRANKLIN's statement "Your argument is sound ... all sound."[3]. Whereas in the first
instance of 'sound' the meaning is synonymous to 'solid', in the repetition the meaning
is reverted and could be translated as 'empty'. This rhetorical strategy is found with
regard to hypertexts on the internet in two slightly different contexts: the first one that
is referred to in the quote by BURBULES is the way in which search engines contextualise
unrelated or even entirely opposite meanings of certain words because of the way they
are constructed and programmed. Although gradually search-engines are becoming more
sensitive to the contexts in which the respective key-words occur, it is still a common
phenomenon that a search on the text-processor program "Latex" also leads to online-
shops offering mattresses as well as to fetish-sites describing their various items.

The second context is the way in which 'antistatis' or 'antanaclasis' are used within a
specific piece of hyperfiction. As in the example above, the author can apply link-triggers
containing a specific word in one context, and then construct the target-frame in such
a way that it is used in an entirely different one. By means of this he can undermine
reader expectations in order to create a certain aesthetic effect, although we can imagine
that an extensive use of antistatical links ultimately leads to the "lost-in-hyperspace"-
phenomenon of incoherence.

3.2.4.6. Link and Sequence-and-Cause-Effect

Links on the internet, in contrast to cross-references in printed literature, "physically"
transport the reader to the fragment that has been chosen as the target-frame by the

---

[2]cf. http://humanities.byu.edu/rhetoric/Figures/A/antistasis.htm, accessed 25.04.05

[3]cf. http://humanities.byu.edu/rhetoric/Figures/A/antanaclasis.htm, accessed 25.04.05

author. In the latter medium, links are merely indicated and it is the reader's decision whether he makes use of it and refers to the target-document, or not.

> [...] because they do not specify or explain such connections, but simply *manifest* them, they are more difficult to recognise and question; often they simply carry the reader with them to inferences that could just as well be drawn quite differently, or could be criticised and rejected. [27, p.115]

Considering what has been said above, it becomes clear that the link as the crucial element of hypertext has many similarities to well-known/classical tropes as provided by literary analysis. As a summary we can state that we have now gained another dimension of analysis by taking into consideration the rhetorical quality of links.

3.3. Interactivity

According to SUTER, reading a hypertext does not involve text-external interaction, i.e. the reader does not really interact with the producer of the text, but only with a (mostly text-based) interface which allows for a restricted degree of interaction. He claims:

> Der Begriff Interaktivität sollte [...] mit Vorsicht verwendet werden, denn was den neuen elektronischen Formen im Vergleich zur herkömmlichen Massenkommunikation eigen ist, bzw. dem Internet allgemein, sind vor allem mehr Auswahlmöglichkeiten (Wahl der Pfade) sowie deutlich mehr Möglichkeiten zur multimedialen Verknüpfung (Dynamisierung). Von Interaktivität kann man nur da wirklich sprechen, wo Menschen mit Menschen, bzw. soziale Wesen miteinander interagieren. [87, p.36]

The act of reading a hypertext requires a high degree of active participation on the part of the reader. He constantly has to build his own paths through the network in order to construct his reading. There are two definitions of interactivity, or rather two degrees of intensity of this concept, which are presented by INTEMANN:

> Für die weitere, umgangssprachliche Interpretation bedeutet Interaktivität, dass auf einem Bildschirm verschiedene Hyperlinks vorhanden sind und der Benutzer das Gefühl hat, er könne frei entscheiden was er lesen oder sehen möchte. Tatsächlich hat er nur die Wahl zwischen verschiedenen vorgegebenen Inhalten. Im engeren Sinn bedeutet interaktiv, dass das System aus *mindestens zwei handelnden Partnern* besteht. Ein Computersystem ist also nur dann wirklich interaktiv, wenn es selbst entscheidet, was der Benutzer auf dem Bildschirm zu sehen bekommt. [46, p.68]

The latter, however, occurs only with artificial intelligence or automated poetry, which are not the subject of this presentation. Furthermore she asks whether interactivity is indeed a typical characteristic of hypertext and states: "Schwache Interaktivität in der

3. Characteristics of Hypertext

dargestellten Form ist also eigentlich kein Merkmal von Hypertext als Konzept, sie ist ein Merkmal elektronischer Plattformen." [46, p.84]. An encyclopedia as a printed manifestation of hypertext, she argues, cannot be regarded as being interactive. The electronic version, however, directly responds to the reader's input and thus fits better into this category. As for the problem of whether all hypertexts are interactive, she concludes:

> Definiert man Interaktivität aber als aufeinander bezogenes Handeln, das Aktivität auf beiden Seiten erfordert, sind nur elektronische Hypertexts interaktiv, da der Computer die Verweisangabe ausführt. In dieser Interpretation ist das Merkmal der Interaktivität unabdingbar verbunden mit der Existenz von Hyperlinks und einem nicht-linearen Systemcharakter. Interaktivität ist das logische Ergebnis aus dem Zusammenspiel aller Merkmale. In diesem Fall wären nicht-elektronische Hypertexts - falls es sie gibt - nicht interaktiv. [46, p.121]

Additionally, BUCHER contributes the concept of 'reversibility' of the interactive process to our examination, and remarks:

> In handlungstheoretischen Klärungen zum Interaktionsbegriff steht ein Kriterium im Mittelpunkt, das Kriterium der Reversibilität: Wenn wir sagen "A interagiert mit B", so heißt das automatisch: "B interagiert mit A". Diese Reversibilität lässt sich so auf die Mensch-Computer-Kommunikation nicht so ohne weiteres übertragen. Jedenfalls würden wir dem Rechnerprogramm nicht in dem Sinne Handlungsfähigkeit einräumen wie den Aktionen des Menschen am Bildschirm. Trotz allem semantischen Widerwillen, die Ausweitung des Begriffs "interaktiv" mitzumachen, bringt sie etwas zum Ausdruck, das für digitale Formen der Medienkommunikation typisch ist: der größere Handlungs- und Entscheidungsspielraum in der Rezeption, verglichen mit den traditionellen linearen Medien Buch, Radio und Fernsehen. [26, p.139]

Thus, although it is clear that the user can influence the progress of the action on screen (at least within the framework that the author/programmer has outlined before), user-interaction with the electronic interface cannot be compared to the sort of interaction involving humans acting and reacting towards each other. In view of the narrative characteristics of hypertext, SEIBEL [76] raises the question whether interactivity and narrativity can exist simultaneously in these texts:

> Im Hinblick auf Interaktivität gilt es also, die Frage zu klären, wie Texte dem Leser zugleich Interaktionsmöglichkeiten bieten können, dennoch aber aufgrund ihrer textuellen Signale das Schema des Narrativen als schematische Superstruktur [...] aktivieren.

In other words, the more the narrative contains interactive elements the reader can connect with, the more problematic the development of the narration becomes. The reason for this is that if the reader takes total control of all the components of the story, there is nothing left which could be 'narrated' to him. This is especially obvious with regard to interactive fiction or computer-games. Here, the player is presented with a basic story ('Spielidee') and moves through the world of the game via his avatar.

3.4. Cross-/Intermediality

Another characteristic of hypertext is 'cross-mediality': A number of works that will be reviewed combine different media and thus benefit from the different channels for conveying information. In *Rice* by GENIWATE [8] for example, the author chooses to incorporate different short films as could be seen on TV or in cinema into her piece of hyperfiction. Likewise, the introductory page of the *wartime project* [14] also uses animated images reminding us of satellite photography of the weather-forecast. Although the primary focus of this project is the literary analysis of hypertexts, it is nevertheless important to be able to account for the narrative properties of cross-medial items in these texts as well. Since the majority of the texts to be analysed consist of elements other than written text, i.e. graphics, video and sound, it must be considered which literary quality these elements contain.

3.4.1. Image-Text Relationships

The idea of combining written text with graphics, however, was performed long before the age of (electronic) hypertext, so this is not in itself an innovation which could entirely be attributed to the area of electronic writing. Romantic poet William BLAKE for instance also produced engravings and paintings, and created books of poetry featuring a poem arranged next to a picture on every double-page.

Another example of this intermedial combination of written texts and graphical elements is the novels by Charles DICKENS, some editions of which also have been richly illustrated. With regard to hyperfiction, it thus becomes clear that in the case of still graphical images, as they can be found on printed paper, these are independent from the medium they are presented on; from the literary point of view it makes no difference whether an edition of BLAKE's poetry, including written text and graphical elements, is presented on the computer screen or on the page. Considerations that could be made here have more to do with accessibility of the text (for an interested reader with a computer and high-speed internet-access, it is easier and quicker to view the text online rather than buying the book or obtaining it from a library) and the physical act of reading itself: reading a nicely-crafted book seems much more comfortable (and thus more enjoyable) than sitting in front of a flickering computer-monitor.

There are other sorts of multi-media elements which are incorporated into works of hyperfiction, which also find their counterpart outside the electronic realm. Although these are mostly and characteristically found in art performances, they are yet again not exclusively restricted to a computerised environment. For instance, we can imagine a poetry reading in which the voice of the poet is accompanied by music, either played on one or more instruments or stemming from a sound recording. Similarly, there could be a video-monitor or a cinema-screen on stage, showing video-sequences as the performance takes place. In pop/rock-concerts, for example, quite often the directors of the show use giant video-screens next to the stage, and project video-sequences onto it on order to accompany the music. In other words, although more effort is necessary to create the impression of an inter-medial literary experience outside the electronic medium, it is by no means impossible. The only difference, therefore, between the work of cross-medial hyperfiction and a multi-media performance is the individual act of receiving the work.

Usually, all these multi-media-additions are used in order to heighten the literary effect and support the narrative by illustrating crucial scenes of the plot or depicting individual characters. There are, however, instances where the graphical supplement actually contradicts the meaning of the written text and thereby creates an interesting ironic tension. One example taken from the area of television is the music-video for the song *Hurra*[4] by German rock-band DIE ÄRZTE: The lyrics of the chorus are:

> [...]
> hip hip hurra! alles ist super, alles ist wunderbar
> hip hip hurra! alles ist besser als es damals war
> alle sind happy, alle sind glücklich, alle sind froh
> und überall, wo man hinguckt: Liebe und Frieden und so
> [...]

---

[4]This song is found on the album *Planet Punk*, produced by Metronome Music GmbH, 1995.

In sharp contrast to the jubilant tone of the passage, the video is produced in a sombre black-and-white style. There are long camera takes on the faces of the members of the band, who have very sad facial expressions and thus caricature the meaning of the lyrics. This diametrical opposition, as we will also see with respect to works of hyperfiction, can be used as a stylistic item quite effectively.

With regard to graphical images, WOLF [95] examines a series of paintings in order to determine whether these contain constituting elements of narratives. He suggests that this is problematic in two respects: Firstly, a still image does not contain any temporal axis ("[...] weitgehende A-Temporalität des bildlichen Mediums [...]" [95, p.54]). And secondly, since a painting can only convey what is visible ("[...] fast ausschließliche[n] Konzentration auf die Repräsentation sichtbarer Oberflächen [...]" [95, p.54]), narrative features such as thoughts and feelings are lacking. Consequently, he suggests:

> Monophasen-Einzelbilder können selbst nicht narrativ im Sinne von geschichten-darstellend sein, sondern bestenfalls Geschichten an Hand einer Plot-Phase an-deuten. Sie haben damit einen relativ geringen Grad an Narrativität. [95, p.73]

In other words, when examining graphical images as isolated entities, it is almost impossible to assign any narrative meaning to them. Hence, including these constituents into our analyses can only yield results when compared to and set against the written texts, i.e. how the graphical elements and pieces of written text coexist and form an aesthetic whole.

Categorisation In a chapter entitled "Show and Tell", McCLOUD [60, pp.153-155] attempts to categorise comics according to the various instances of written text combined with images:

Word specific combination [...] pictures illustrate, but don't significantly add to a largely complete text [...]

Picture specific combination [...] words do little more than add a soundtrack to a visually told sequence [...]

Duo-specific combination [...] both words and pictures send essentially the same message [...]

Additive combination [...] words amplify or elaborate on an image or vice versa [...]

Parallel combinations [...] words and pictures seem to follow very different courses – without intersecting [...]

Montage [...] words are treated as integral parts of the picture [...]

Interdependent combinations [...] words and pictures go hand in hand to convey an idea that neither could convey alone [...]

Although the author develops these categories in view of the genre of comics, I suggest they are nevertheless quite useful for our analysis of hypertexts as well, since, as we have seen, the two genres have much in common. Consequently, the individual categories developed above will also be included in our model in order to be able to suitably describe the possible implications of image-text relationships.

3.4.2. Sound-Text Relationships

Another instance of intermediality of works of hypertextual fiction is the occurrence of sound. This can either be permanent background noise, a piece of music or sound-effects that are triggered by the user's actions. As with cinema, the artistic use of sound is an integral part of some works of hyperfiction, so I would like to point out the implications quite briefly here.

Keeping in mind the large amount of production software and the ample sources of documentation and user-support, for the author to incorporate a specific sound-file into a work is, technically speaking, very easy. The internet provides a vast amount of sound-files and recordings that exist on other media, i.e. CDs or vinyl-records, can be digitalised and integrated into the work without much effort. Nor does the kind of sound-recording really matter in this respect, since all variations can be obtained with relative ease, be it recordings of an old speech, background-noise of a scene in the street or an exotic piece of music. In other words, an author of electronic texts has got nearly unrestricted access to various sounds that he can make use of for his work, in order to gain the desired artistic effect.[5]

3.4.3. Film

So far we have taken a glimpse at the way in which written text and intermedial items - animated or still - are combined to form an artistic whole. In this respect, it is almost self-evident to refer to a neighboring discipline which by definition deals with various occurrences of images and sound: film-studies. How and what do images and sequences of images mean? What additional information is contained in the artistic combination of different layers of information? Although it is not possible to refer to film-studies in greater detail - since after all this project would like to concern itself mainly with the literary properties of hypertexts - I nevertheless deem it important to refer to these studies in some detail because - as we will see with regard to the example *obituaries.count* [4] - filmic elements are often presented in works of hyperfiction.

Interestingly, with regard to the coexistence of the layers of information just mentioned, the origins of modern cinema already contained some of the markers of modern hypertexts we are discussing. Before it was technologically feasible to add sound to films, film-makers had to deliver the plot without making use of the actors' voices. Thus, the action was furthered by gestures and mimics, but also by still images pasted between the individual scenes containing written text, either in the form of commentary to the film or extracts of dialogues. Thus, in a very basic form, directors used this technique in order to make up for the lack of technological means for conserving the actors' voices on the filmic tape as well.

As has been mentioned before in Chapter 3.1 on linearity, cinema is a very sequential medium, containing no possibility for the reader/viewer to interact. In fact, one

---

[5]The only restrictions in this respect are copyright-issues.

can hardly imagine a medium which is more sequential: the audience is exposed to the sequence of images that is being projected, the film is physically stored on a reel running from beginning to end. However, the cinematic coexistence of moving images and intersected tabloids containing written text bears resemblances to the hypertexts in question. But not only this combination, but the pure sequence of images contains room for interpretation which we have to explore for our purposes.

Mise-en-scène In other words, a specific instance of a hypertextual work could also be suitably described by using various categories from film theory. In this respect, a useful descriptive category is the so-called 'mise-en-scène': The arrangement of figures and objects within one frame/shot. This concept, which originally derives from the area of theatre-production, is the basis for the aesthetic effect of the film itself. According to GIANNETTI, there are several aspects of 'mise-en-scène' which I will give a brief outline of at this stage. As will become evident, the same aspects that help film theorists to describe, interpret and classify a given film, are also quite valuable for the analysis of hypertextual fiction. Similar to all constituents of a movie-scene purposefully arranged on the big theatre-screen, the hypertext author arranges the bits and different layers of information his work is made of on the computer screen.[6]

Although a "[...] single-frame image from a movie [...] is necessarily an artificially frozen moment which was never intended to be wrenched from its context in time and motion [...]"[44], it nevertheless serves to analyse the overall work by depicting the characteristics of the fragments it consists of. Each single image of a film is contained in and confined by the frame. On the celluloid-tape, this is typically the width of the material, and accordingly, the projected image on the movie screen. GIANNETTI points out that the aspect ratio of the projected image is important for the aesthetic effect of the film. With reference to *2001: A Space Odyssey* by Stanley KUBRICK, he argues that

---

[6]The similarity becomes even more obvious when the hypertext is projected onto a larger screen, which nowadays is quite an easy thing to do, using a so-called beamer.

the effect of this particular film for a great part relies on the wide-screen because this is especially suitable for showing space's vastness. Discussing the transfer to a smaller screen he argues that if "[...] this image were cropped to a conventional aspect ratio [...] much of the feel of the infinity of space would be sacrificed." [44, p.50]

Similarly, this holds true for hypertextual works. Modern computers are shipped and installed with a variety of monitor sizes and screen resolutions. Depending on the hardware the reader is using to enjoy a piece of hypertextual fiction, his actual reading experience is altered. In contrast to the film-director, the author of such a work has no control over the frame of his work. Although some authors often suggest "best read on a screen with 1024 x 768 resolution", it is nevertheless possible to access the work using a smaller or higher resolution. In other words, the author loses one organising principle of the 'mise-en-scène' to a certain extent.

But not only the physical space of the frame itself is important. Following GIANNETTI [44, p.53], the arrangement of characters or objects within the frame can also carry metaphoric and symbolic meaning: "Placement within the frame is another instance of how form is actually content. Each of the major portions of the frame - centre, top, bottom, and edges - can be exploited for such symbolic and metaphoric purposes." The centre of the frame, for instance, typically suggests special importance or interest, the camera usually focuses on items of characters which are forwarding the plot or explaining and commenting on the story. Things arranged near to the top usually suggest power and authority, things at the bottom are likely to be regarded as weak and inferior. Yet again, there exist obvious resemblances to hypertextual fiction, because also in this medium the arrangement of all visual items determines the way the work as such is perceived and interpreted. Here, like a film director, the author has full control over the distribution of different fragments on the screen, except for the fact that because of smaller or larger screen-resolutions the items are reshuffled or do not appear to the reader at all.

obituaries.count   As an example of a piece of hyperfiction resembling a film in that it permits no user-interaction at all, I would like to briefly discuss *obituaries.count* by Claudia LOMELI BUYOLI.

Figure 3.1.

" obituaries.count"

This piece skillfully plays with a limited number of artistic items, which contribute to quite an intense work of art. As we will see shortly, it differs very much from other hyperfictional works in that it contains no links and no user-interaction at all. Although there are indeed different textual fragments in the "Flash"-film[7], they are all randomly looped through, so that there is no possibility of interaction between the reader and the text. The latter, therefore, could more suitably described as being linear, even though because of the randomness, the ground structure seems more like a jumping back and forth, but these are only internal jumps made by the program. The work uses a text-form which originally stems from (printed) newspapers and for newspaper-readers is an item belonging to every-day-life. Since the design and the contents of obituaries are so well-known, the author has got the possibility to use this knowledge as a basis for a

---

[7]cf. Chapter 4 on technology

parody.

What the user sees is a black-and-white, rectangular obituary in the middle of the computer screen which addresses the victims of the last Iraq war. By letting the languages and the meaning the textual fragments create fluctuate, the author emphasises the fact that obituaries are a global phenomenon, the rhetorics of which are replaceable and interchangeable regardless of where these are being written or read. The date of the obituary is always the same as the actual date the text is read on, thus the text gains the quality of actuality and credibility at the same time. Furthermore, in order to increase the desired artistic effect, the author has put a body-count at the bottom of the page, which is incremented roughly every second. Furthermore, there are strong sounds of war, such as machine-gun fire, and screams of women and children in the background.

It follows that it is possible to analyse a given work on two different levels. At one level, we can identify the individual layers the works consist of, such as a movie-clip which is inserted into such a work would be analysed as an isolated entity. Then, at a second level, we can scrutinise the overall picture and the meaning that is conveyed by the arrangement and the combination of the different items.

Further interesting categories of film-studies which could be applied to hypertexts, but would be clearly beyond the scope of this presentation, are the areas of 'film-semiotics' and the concept of 'montage'. These aspects are thoroughly discussed - apart from others - by French theorist Christian METZ[8].

---

[8] *Sprache und Film*, Athenäum Verlag, Frankfurt am Main 1973, and *Semiologie des Films*, Wilhelm Fink Verlag, München, 1972.

3.5. Intertextuality

Intertextuality is also one of the vital characteristics of hypertext because of the ease with which one can establish permanent links between two or more works of hyperfiction. Taking a non-literary example, a general entry on the Victorian era in an online reference[9] work might contain a link to a biography of Charles DICKENS, which in turn could contain a link to a short extract from *Oliver Twist*[10]. For this reason, I would like to discuss the concept in some detail and show on what different levels intertextuality can be traced in fictional hypertexts, and, from a literary perspective, how this can be used in order to develop a narrative.

In a hyperfictional work, authors achieve the desired aesthetic effects by combining various textual elements and interlink them in a meaningful way. Relationships between texts, thus, are established between these individual fragments and the context they occur in. Also, external links can be integrated, connecting the narrative to similar works surrounding it. If we take a look at the interface[11] the reader uses in order to access the text, there are also quite a number of links which are always present: A click on the browser's 'home'-button for instance takes the reader back to a predetermined default-page, in other words, even the interface itself carries some intertextual implications.

The horizontal axis of Intertextuality Analysis is the link between author and reader, who gets quoted or summarized and author interpretations in network of relationships between textual utterances (images too) and other texts (references, citations, quotes, summaries). There is an ongoing dynamic textual production process, of which each utterance and the text itself is a moment. I call this historicity, you may prefer to call it citation. It is how the text is designed and constructed and produced as an intertext or tapestry. There is also a second axis you can analyze, the vertical which is the context of each utterance in a text that draws it into its intertextual web (e.g. by irony, satire, juxtaposition).[23]

---

[9]Cf. Chapter 2.4.3.4.
[10]Cf. more detailed discussion in chapter 2.4.3.4.
[11]Cf. chapter 4.1 for a thorough discussion of the 'interface'.

3. Characteristics of Hypertext

Intertextuality in the sense that Julia KRISTEVA (cf. [54]) has proposed relates to the fact that all the writing that was and is produced either implicitly or explicitly refers to other texts. During the actual production-process, the author might be quite unaware of the fact, but in theory, all the texts that he receives or has received potentially leave traces in his writing. Here, it can be argued that since the author could more suitably be described as only restructuring existing material, arguably he disappears to a certain extent as authority over 'his' genuine text.

> Kristevas auf die "Dezentrierung des Subjekts" gerichtete Konzeption löst den Autos als Instanz ab. Sie enthält den Gedanken, dass sich Texte subjektlos permanent selbst absorbieren, transformieren, produzieren und reproduzieren und damit völlig offen bleiben. [49, p.15]

JAKOBS argues that the term has been overused in the past having led to quite a range of connotations as a consequence. For this reason, she suggests the following subdivision of 'intertextuality' [49, pp.16-19]. First of all, she establishes the two main categories of either intertextuality as a 'general attribute' ('allgemeines Merkmal') or a 'special attribute' ('spezielles Merkmal'). Regarding the first category, she establishes the following subcategories:

- Intertextualität als Wissensbasis für die Rezeption und Produktion von Texten [...]

- Generische Intertextualität

- Translatorische Intertextualität

- Produktiv bedingte Intertextualität

The first category, according to the author, concerns both the production- and the reception-sides of texts. For the author as well as for the reader it is necessary to be familiar with similar texts, in other words, in order for the information-transfer from sender to receiver to function, both sides must have the same knowledge-base. As far as 'generic intertextuality' is concerned, the author states that it is because of recurring themes and patterns that we can identify intertextuality, which in this sense works as a basis for typological considerations. This category is also related to the next one, namely 'translatory intertextuality'. Here, JAKOBS suggests that transferring textual patterns into another language also represents a case of intertextuality, since the source text and the resulting translation are interrelated.

Finally, regarding intertextuality as a general characteristic, the author enumerates intertextuality resulting from the actual production process. At the core of this class is the assumption that texts can be viewed as open constructs that can be continually amended, which is a perspective that will also be discussed further in Chapter 3.6 on the relationship between open and closed hypertext systems. In other words, each text, especially when it exists in an electronic environment, as in a computer text-processor program for example, can be altered quite easily; its individual structural features, according to this perspective, could be regarded as points of departure for other, new texts. Therefore, since a text always oscillates between its final physical manifestation and its potential for creating and nurturing new texts, it can be called intertextual.

As far as the second main category is concerned, JAKOBS traces the following classes:

- Kooperative Intertextualität
- Transformierende Intertextualität
- Deiktische Intertextualität

With regard to the first category, the author aims at describing those kind of texts that are inherently 'dialogic' in that they can stimulate responses to them. Here, JAKOBS gives the example of a letter, which according to her requires a response in the same text form. Yet again, this descriptive category quite fittingly accounts for hypertexts. Collaborative writing projects, for instance, contain these 'dialogic' elements, which is the reason they work in the first place: an author describes the starting-point of a plot within a few hypertext fragments, and invites the visitors/readers to become writers themselves and continue the plot. Hence, the readers enter a dialogue with the author through their contributions of further plot-developments; this example on the

3. *Characteristics of Hypertext*

one hand refers to the class of 'cooperative intertextuality', on the other, it also bears characteristics of interactivity, which we have discussed in detail before in Chapter 3.3.

'Transforming intertextuality' refers to the phenomenon that occurs when an altered version is deduced from an original source text and thus takes a different form. This occurs for instance when a story is being retold: in this case, not only a second version of an original text is created, but at the same time it has been transferred from the written to an oral environment.

Finally, the last class the author contributes to the discussion in this context is 'deictic intertextuality', and I suggest that most of the hypertexts we encounter on the internet can be described according to this category.

> [Deiktische Intertextualität] liege vor, wenn ein "Texterzeuger aus einem vorange-
> gangenen Text etwas (einen versprachlichten Begriff, ein Zitat u.ä.) aufgreift oder
> in ähnlicher Weise auf einen kommenden Text, einen meist von ihm selbst später
> beabsichtigten Text, hinweist, einen Vorverweis in seinen Text einführt" [...][49,
> p.21]

'Deixis' is defined by SCHMAUKS [74, p.81] as "[...] die situationsabhängige Referenz auf Elemente der Rahmensituation eines Kommunikationsvorgangs durch verbale und nonverbale Mittel." Hence, in connection with our discussion of various classes of intertextuality, the linguistic category of 'deixis' emphasises the importance of the overall context for the respective text. According to the definition quoted above, deictic intertextuality can be understood to radiate in two directions, namely both into the direction of already established texts, and into the direction of future texts. This backward- and forward-feature, in my opinion, describes the way in which the internet and, as a direct result, fictional hypertexts are constructed. The author inserts different texts - both produced by him and by others - into his work by means of linking to them and thus creating intertextual relationships. In this sense, he also situates the individual elements of his work of hyperfiction within the larger context of the hypertextual network he has created.

3. Characteristics of Hypertext

These considerations also have implications for the production of a work of hyperfiction. While it is accomplished very easily to integrate a foreign text into one's own by simply linking to it on the internet, this is not possible in the same manner with regard to the 'offline'- or 'CD-ROM hypertexts' mentioned above in Chapter 2.4.3.3. Distributing a work of hyperfiction on such a data medium means that every text one would like to refer to in one's work needs to be copied and put on the same medium, which potentially opens up questions of copyright.

As we have seen, in order to substantiate the claim that one of the most prominent characteristics of hypertexts is intertextuality, one needs to highlight its various implications and occurrences.

3.6. Open vs. Closed Texts

A very important characteristic of hypertexts is the fact that because of the electronic medium it is both very easy to amend and edit the text and to blend it with other surrounding texts. As far as the number of textual fragments which constitute the main body of text is concerned, theorists differentiate between open/dynamic and closed/static hypertexts. STORRER [84, pp.15-16], for example argues:

> *Geschlossene Hypertextsysteme* verfügen über eine feste Anzahl von Modulen. Auch wenn sie durch externe Links in größere Hypertextsysteme [...] eingebunden sind, sind sie konzipiert als statische Produkte mit stabiler Struktur, auf die spätere Produkte ohne Risiko Bezug nehmen können [...] *Offene Hypertexte* dagegen haben "offene Enden" [...] Die Module können aktualisiert werden, neue Module und Links können dazu kommen.

According to the author it is possible to find texts that are static, i.e. not changeable anymore, and texts that are dynamically and continuously growing, because there is the possibility for the readers to add their own fragments to these structures. There are numerous examples of these collaborative writing projects. These seem to be the type of hypertext that mostly subscribes to the interactive and immediate transfer of information made possible by the internet. Internet-users who do not know each other and live in very distant places around the world find one platform to communicate with each other and contribute to the artwork as a whole. Still, the majority of fictional hypertexts on the internet represents closed structures and are identifiable as such, so I agree with INTEMANN in that in order to make a text tangible (and analysable) one needs to establish its borders thus separate it from others. Without doing so, the whole internet might be seen as one gigantic text; and while this is certainly an interesting point of view regarding all the intertextual implications this might have, it nevertheless makes analyses of individual works nearly impossible.

3.6.1. Text Boundaries

The fragmented internal organisation of most hypertexts, in addition, challenges our understanding of text-borders. In view of a dynamic and potentially unstable text, how do we know for sure what is still part of one text and what already belongs to a neighbouring one? Robert KENDALL, one of the creators of the ELECTRONIC LITERATURE ORGANISATION DIRECTORY, makes the following point:

> In print publishing the physical containment of a work within a set of covers generally makes it easy to distinguish the boundaries of that work. These boundaries are more likely to become blurred on the Web. It may also be hard to determine whether a site consists of a single multisection work that should constitute a single entry or several discrete works that should be entered individually. [...] [52, pp.3-4]

The 'openness' of hypertext has also implications for the act of reading itself. If the reader enters a work of hyperfiction, it is much harder for him to obtain exact knowledge as to where exactly in the structure he is positioned. Here, navigational tools and other structural guides are necessary for the reader not to lose his orientation. In contrast, when regarding a novel published in the form of a printed book, it is possible at every stage of the reading to check how many pages have been read and how many pages there are left.

A consequence of this is that categories such as 'introduction' and especially 'ending' need to be discussed again. While it poses a relatively small problem to trace the beginning of a hypertext - most texts offer an 'official' starting-page - it is problematic to make exact statements as to the respective endings. In a printed work, the discourse irreversibly stops at the last page, whereas in a piece of hyperfiction containing links in every module, the reading potentially never ceases. In the context of her close readings of *afternoon - a story*, DOUGLAS [38, p.164] tries to approach the question of the identifiability of endings as follows:

> What triggers the ending of a reading? Where print readers encounter texts already supplied with closure and endings, readers of interactive fiction generally

must supply their own sense of an ending. This affords us a new understanding of the relationship between the structures integral to the act of reading and the concept of closure. What prompts readers to decide they are "finished" with a particular interactive narrative and to discontinue their readings of it?

Her solution to the question, however, is unfortunately a rather vague and subjective suggestion based on her own multiple readings of *afternoon - a story*:

> Our sense of arriving at closure is satisfied when we manage to resolve narrative tensions and to minimize ambiguities, to explain puzzles, and to incorporate as many of the narrative elements into a coherent pattern - preferably one for which we have a script gleaned from either life experience or encounters with other narratives. [38, p.185]

It seems, therefore, necessary to develop a systematic approach to the question how endings are constructed. While the development of such a model is far beyond the scope of this research, first steps are being made by the *Aachen* research group on the subject of endings.[12]

Reception and Coherence   Together with the subject of text-borders we also have to refer to another question which regards the way in which hypertexts are received by the reader:

> A literary text must [...] be conceived in such a way that it will engage the reader's imagination in the task of working things out for himself, for reading is only a pleasure when it is active and creative. [47]

Wolfgang ISER postulates that in order for the reader to enjoy a specific text, he needs to deal with the text actively and create his own coherent reading (or readings). He suggests that a text contains 'blanks' or 'gaps' between certain narrative segments which the reader has to fill in order to create 'meaning'. With regard to these gaps,

---

[12]Forschungs-Projekt "'Ends and Endings': Zur Struktur von Schlüssen in Literatur und Kultur", `http://www.rwth-aachen.de/anglistik/de/angl1/research/pro_endings.htm`, accessed 25.04.05

3. Characteristics of Hypertext

MILLER argues that they "[...] can only exist within a structure which is presumed to be otherwise coherent: gaps have to be *gaps-in-something*." [62] In other words, since the narrative closure - in face of unclear text boundaries and multiple reading paths - cannot be taken for granted anymore, it also becomes quite a difficult task to fill in the blanks that are provided by the discourse. According to the author, this is even more problematic because a hypertext usually provides so many gaps that the reader will either give up reading or not actively engage in creating his own reading but rather switch to another textual fragment:

> Ultimately, by foregrounding gaps, hyperfiction diminishes the significance readers assign to the words on the screen. The conventional reader response to puzzlement in a hyperfiction is not to read the words in front of you more carefully, but with a mouse click to exchange them for new ones. Because each piece of hypertext presents itself as a question to which the reader knows there is no answer, the reader soon becomes discouraged from doing the hard work of looking for answers. [62]

The 'openness' of hypertext can also be understood in another context. INTEMANN [46, p.99] refers to the relationship between static single author projects and dynamically growing and potentially 'open' collaborative writing projects. She suggests:

> [...] Die Frage der offenen Textgrenzen lässt sich demnach nicht für Hypertext generell beantworten. Es gibt Hypertextsorten mit offenen Grenzen, aber es gibt auch geschlossene Hypertextsysteme. Das Merkmal "offene Textgrenzen" kann also nicht als allgemein gültig für die Definition von Hypertext angenommen werden.

Undoubtedly, the 'open' texts in this sense - almost by definition - are bound to be more complex since they are continually growing. An academic study, therefore, is only imaginable when referring to individual "snapshots" of respective stages of production. The author lays a foundation for the text that other participants then build on and develop further. However, the results and the directions of this development largely remain unknown and unpredictable. In view of these projects, AMERIKA [79] remarks:

3. Characteristics of Hypertext

In fact, the more I think about it, narrative and authorship, [sic] don't even feel like the right terms here. It feels more like process-oriented network art that has a story to it, an ongoing ungoing story, we might say, although this should not be misconstrued with the sort of anything-goes, anyone-can-contribute, pseudo-utopian ideal of the Network as Author, since we all know that most of the projects that grow out of that false logic are, for the most part, uninteresting experiments in what ends up being chat-discussions camouflaged as fictitious discourses procured by hapless participants.

For this reason, this presentation will deal with 'closed' texts in particular, meaning that there are a fixed number of fragments that make out the work and can be analysed individually. Only if these sorts of texts are academically accounted for does it seem possible to move on to 'open' structures such as collaborative writing-projects as a next step.

In another sense, this dissertation will be concerned with 'open structures', namely concerning the question of unclear text borders.

3.7. Authorship vs. Readership

> Als permanenter Mitarbeiter am Text pendelt der Hypertext-Leser zwischen seiner
> Freiheit, sich selbständig zusammenzulesen, was er will, und seiner Funktion als
> diskursiver Kohärenzstifter, die ihn für seine Lektüre verantwortlich macht. Diese
> Rolle entspricht der des Herausgebers, der als erster Leser und zweiter Autor,
> Geschriebenes sammelt, bearbeitet und herausgibt [...][93, pp.32-33]

When discussing the development of a new genre which is technologically and aesthe-
tically different from traditional forms of reading and writing, it is important to reflect
the notions of the production and the reception of literature as they are traditionally
conceived. As LANDOW argues, "[w]e still read *according* to print technology [...]."
[55, p.57] Furthermore, he doubts the applicability of the term 'reader' for individuals
receiving hypertexts:

> Additional problems arise when one considers that hypertext involves a more
> active reader, one who not only chooses her reading paths but also has the op-
> portunity of reading as an author; at any time, the person reading can assume
> an authorial role by attaching links or adding material to the text being read.
> Therefore, a term like *reader* [...] does not seem appropriate. [55, p.57]

3.7.1. Producing Hypertexts

Hypertext theorists have often argued that the production-side of hypertext qualifies for
what BARTHES postulated as the "Death of the Author", namely the focussing away
from the literary "genius" of the author towards the text he has produced and behind
which he has to "disappear" necessarily once the text has been manifested.[13] LANDOW

---

[13] "The Author, when we believe in him, is always conceived as the past of his own book: book and
author are voluntarily placed on one and the same line, distributed as a *before* and an *after*: the
Author is supposed to *feed* the book, i.e. he lives before it, thinks, suffers, lives for it; he has the
same relation of antecedence with his work that a father sustains with his child. Quite the contrary,
the modern *scriptor* is born *at the same time* as his text; he is not furnished with a being which
precedes or exceeds his writing, he is not the subject of which his books would be the predicate;

for instance claims that readers at the same time become writers constructing their own text by using the navigational tools at hand - "[...] the functions of reader and writer become more deeply entwined with each other than ever before." [55, p.90]. The more divergent readings are produced by the flexible and non-sequential arrangement of lexias in a hypertext, the more control the author loses according to this line of argument.

I believe that with regard to hypertext fiction on the internet, quite the contrary is actually true. Firstly, the links within the respective work are not randomly chosen by a computer-program but intentionally placed by the author. The 'controlling-process', however, begins even earlier, when the author decides which of the numerous publishing technologies at hand he would like to use in the creative process. This is something writers of traditional printed literature are only marginally exposed to - their books are being published by professional publishing houses, and the influence the writer has on the actual product is often limited. Moreover, I suggest that when the writer of traditional fiction has handed in his manuscript and has his work published, it is finished unless he decides to publish a revised version. In contrast, a hypertext author virtually never sees the ultimate completion of his work, he might decide to alter parts of his textual framework and he needs to make sure that his work can be accessed all times. For instance, it is necessary for him to take care of storage of the work as well. If there are server down-times or software-problems, his work cannot be accessed temporarily, and - even worse - if the respective hard-disk crashes and the author has failed to back-up, the work is irretrievably lost.

In other words, the author is still very much present in hypertext fiction, in addition to being a creative writer he has to be familiar with the underlying programming as well as the publication-methods on the internet in order to be able to present his work.

Referencing As far as the production process is concerned, critics have often indicated that because of insufficient bibliographical information, it is problematic to attribute

---

there is no time other than that of the speech-act, and every text is written eternally *here* and *now.*" [22, pp.52ff]

works to authors and vice versa. Moreover, dates of publication are more difficult to make clear statements about because given the effortless revisability of the works in question, a single work can have several publication dates as authors might decide to re-upload their works in slightly altered form. Finally, the fact that websites can easily be moved to new locations makes referencing a problem because links that target a specific website are not updated (at least not automatically) each time such a move occurs. As a consequence, so-called 'dead links' make the identification of works problematic. For these reasons, academic study and acknowledgement also become more difficult. KENDALL [52, p.3] comments:

> Obtaining accurate author attributions, publisher names, and publication dates
> for Web publications can be surprisingly difficult, because this information is of-
> ten ambiguous, incomplete, or difficult to find on the Web sites where the works
> themselves are published.

My research, however, will show that authors of hyperfiction on the internet become successively aware of these problematics. Consequently, almost all of the works the corpus comprises contain exact bibliographical data on the initial pages to emphasise their "stable" presence on the internet.

3.7.2. Reading Hypertexts

> "Ich kann nicht mehr" hat sich der Medienforscher Bernd Wingert bei der Lektüre
> von *Afternoon* gesagt, obwohl er sich vorgenommen hatte, die ganze Hyperfik-
> tion zu lesen. "Nach stundenlangem Explorieren, Lesen, Zusammenstellen von
> Karten, Übersetzen, Anfertigen von Notizen zur Erzählstruktur, dem Abwandern
> von Pfaden, dem Lesen von Rezensionen und der freundlichen Unterstützung von
> Kollegen, um deren Leseerfahrungen einzuholen [...] neige ich zu dem Urteil, daß
> [...] Afternoon nicht funktioniert." [68, p.332]

This statement refers to Michael JOYCE's canonical work *afternoon - a story*. With regard to the reception of elaborate and rhizomatic hypertexts, there seems to be a specific threshold where the narration becomes incoherent and as such is no longer enjoyable. Although the works of hyperfiction we will be primarily assessing in the course of this presentation are mostly less complex, there is still the lurking danger that the author puts too much strain on the coherence-building capabilities of his readers. This is also mirrored in the statement by DOUGLAS [37, p.117] referring to Michael JOYCE's *WOE*:

> The nature of the medium has the narrative hurling down a gauntlet the moment I begin: no gentle induction into the narrative flow, no subtle introductions of the dramatis personae, no suggestive unravelling of the diegetic ball of yarn. Instead, I am confronted simultaneously with the necessity of discovering the characters, their identities, situations, and how I can expect the narrative to come together with a sense of temporary bewilderment of what composition theorists call the "all-at-once-ness" of the act of writing, the distinct sensation of cognitive overload from tackling too many textual strata at once.

It is obligatory for the reader to build a complex mental map while clicking through the network of fragments. The more possibilities for selection there are, the more the reader has to get involved in order to develop a coherent reading. Here, the degree of mental effort necessary to produce 'sense' varies recognisably. In a complex rhizomatic structure, the amount of processing of gaps can in fact be quite a laborious task, which is why some of these texts become almost impossible to process; due to their structure, the readers experience a cognitive overload and stop reading because of sheer tiredness.

The question whether closure is achieved to a reasonable level is the center of studies of so-called "web-site usability". Here, in an experimental set-up, individual users are asked to use a specific internet-site and perform various tasks on its basis. By monitoring the users' behaviour, it is then possible to make valid statements as to the quality of the overall arrangement of the site, especially its navigational elements. A work of hyperfiction experimenting with these conventions is *IN MEMORY DO WE TRUST?*, which will be examined in Chapter 6.8.

3.8. Models

Resulting from the different characteristics attributable to hypertexts, I would like to present two models which serve both as a summary to what has been discussed before as well as the fundament for our analytical toolkit.

3.8.1. Model I: Suter

This approach has been developed by Swiss scholar Beat SUTER [87], who has introduced a number of categories based on the internal logical structure of hypertexts. Put simply, the causal structure is determined by cause-and-effect patterns throughout the story. As a principle of organising the text, hypertext adds quite an interesting dimension to this structure, since the reader/user is given the opportunity to manipulate the causal structure by making conscious decisions when clicking a specific link for example. SUTER suggests the following organisational types:

Axial(linear) This structural mode, according to SUTER, mostly resembles the way in which print literature is read since the invention of the printing press (although, as we have seen, the printed book is a non-sequential medium). Here, the reader starts at one fixed point in order to make his way through the text successively until he has reached a fixed ending. He is only given the choice to move away from this axis temporarily, as in the reading of footnotes. However, these side-branches never go any further and thus never open up different alternatives for the narrative; the reader needs to go back to the point where he has branched off and continue to move along the main axis.

Tentacle This structure is characterised by multiple axes the reader can move on. Beginning in one root, the reader has to decide at a very early stage which path he would like to follow until the end of the narrative. Once he has decided on a path, he has no other chance to move to another axis, there are no interconnections between the "tentacles". The only theoretical chance to explore the other story-lines would be to return to the very beginning of the story and pick a different strand.

Tree-structure A more complex structural model is the so called tree-structure, which is most importantly characterised by its hierarchical order. Similar to the tentacle, there are several branches the plot develops on. However, in contrast to the former, the reader is provided with a number of choices at every node. In other words, the reader moves down the hierarchy to access successively finer subbranches until he has reached the predetermined ending. In case he wants to follow another strand, he only has to go back to the preceding knot in order to enter a new side-branch.

Maze A maze or labyrinthine structure is characterised by it having two points which can either serve as an entry or an exit. Once the reader has chosen where to start, he moves through the structure, encountering numerous possibilities to decide on his path. Some of his decisions - as in a real labyrinth - will lead into dead ends, some will carry him further until he finally reaches the predetermined exit. Readings of different readers will only differ in that they might encounter lexias in a different order along the way. The solution of the narrative, however, always remains the same.

Net/rhizome The rhizome can be regarded as the most "open" structural variant. Here, one recognises multiple entry- and exit-points, the structure has no specific frame, rather it moves and grows in every direction. Individual textual fragments are highly interconnected and the reading experience puts a high cognitive load on the reader, who never experiences a sense of having mastered the whole work, at least not in the traditional sense.

Multiple rhizome Finally, the multiple rhizome enlarges the idea of the rhizome, in that a specific fragment of the main rhizome triggers another minor rhizome which can be moved through before coming back to the original one.

3.8.2. Model II: Aarseth

Norwegian scholar Espen AARSETH, in his highly influential book *Cybertext*, develops a range of categories to create an inventory of what he calls 'ergodic texts'. Interestingly, he does not limit himself to purely electronic texts, but includes every work that requires "nontrivial effort [...] to allow the reader to traverse the text [...]" [18, p.1]. These include traditional printed literature such as the Chinese *I Ching* and NABOKOV's *Pale Fire* as well as digital texts such as the offline-hyperfiction *Victory Garden* by MOULTHROP and the interactive computer-game *Adventure*. For his model he establishes the following terminology:

> [...] It is useful to distinguish between strings as they appear to readers and strings as they exist in the text, since these may not always be the same. For want of better terms, I call the former *scriptons* and the latter *textons* [...] In addition to textons and scriptons, a text consists of what I call a traversal function - the mechanism by which scriptons are revealed or generated from textons and presented to the user of the text. [18, p.62]

Regarding scriptons, the author adds that 'scriptons' for him are what an "[...]'ideal reader' reads by strictly following the linear structure of the textual output." [18, p.62][14] In view of the broad spectrum of works the author chooses for his analysis, I suggest that some of his categories are not entirely applicable regarding the narrower corpus of primary material this research is concerned with. In the following, I would like to present AARSETH's [18, pp.63-64] categories briefly and at the same time examine their usefulness for our purposes.

Dynamics: "In a static text the scriptons are constant; in a dynamic text the contents of scriptons may change while the number of textons remains fixed (intratextonic dynamics, or IDT), or the number (and content) of textons may vary as well (textonic dynamics, or TDT) [...]" While the author refers to JOYCE's *afternoon - a story* as an example for a static text, we can replace this CD-ROM hypertext with every piece of internet hypertext this research is concerned with. As the author argues, computer-games or multi-user games can be classified as being dynamic because

---

[14]Cf. Chapter 3.1 for a further discussion of linearity and the differentiations between the ground- and the surface-structure of a text

the relationship of scriptons and textons varies. In hyperfictional works, however, the relationship is always static, because the scriptons are 1:1 representations of the textons building the ground structure. As a consequence, this is also true for collaborative writing projects which allow readers to contribute fragments to the work, because every texton which is being added finds its actualised counterpart - the scripton.

Consequently, since in my opinion this analytical category will not yield interesting results with regard to our corpus, I will not include them in our analytical matrix.

Determinability: "This variable concerns the stability of the traversal function; a text is determinate if the adjacent scriptons of every scripton are always the same; if not, the text is indeterminate [...]". Here, the author reflects on the occurrence of randomness in ergodic works. While for computer-games the effect of chance is often vital, in hyperfiction it is quite rare. However, since the authors of *The Unknown* and *kokura* have used subtle randomness in their works, we will include this category into our model.

Transiency: "If the mere passing of the user's time causes scriptons to appear, the text is transient; if not, it is intransient [...]". This category refers to the degree of user-participation or interactivity a given text offers, and is therefore vital for the closer analysis of our corpus. We will see that authors often integrate parts into their work which are forwarded automatically - such as a film-sequence for instance - in order to slow down the discourse and emphasise a certain point. Others, like LIALINA in *My Boyfriend came back from the War*, completely do without these transient parts and stress the importance of the reader's engagement.

Perspective: "If the text requires the user to play a strategic role as a character in the world described by the text, then the text's perspective is personal; if not, then it is impersonal [...]". With regard to this category, the author specifically refers to computer-games, where the reader can direct his character ('avatar') through the fictional story-world, deciding on its fate as the narrative proceeds. Almost by definition, however, this degree of personal participation does not occur in hyperfiction, which is the reason why this category will not be included in the analytical toolset.

Access: "If all scriptons of the text are readily available to the user at all times, then the text is random access (typically the codex); if not, then access is controlled [...]". This category reflects the different methods of enabling the reader to navigate through a hypertext. Since a work's readability and coherence ultimately rely on effective means of browsing, this category is very relevant in the context of this dissertation. Therefore, we will include it into our model to be able to examine the different strategies the authors provide for their works to be traversed, especially navigational tools.

Linking: "A text may be organized by explicit links for the user to follow, conditional links that can only be followed if certain conditions are met, or by none of these (no links) [...]". Connected to the navigational properties of a hypertext is the question which functions links perform in the construction of a work. The interconnections of lexias, which were also referred to in detail in Chapter 3.2.4, are of vital importance for the overall effect of a given work and because of this also appear in our model.

User functions: "Besides the interpretative function of the user, which is present in all texts, the use of some texts may be described in terms of additional functions: the explorative function, in which the user must decide which part to take, and the configurative function, in which scriptons are in part chosen or created by the user. If textons or traversal functions can be (permanently) added to the text, the user function is textonic." The last function the author develops reflects the fact that in some digital texts the user can actively modify the textons or add new ones to the already existing framework. A good example of this are the so called 'collaborative writing projects', which are 'open texts' in the sense we have discussed in Chapter 3.6. However, since this dissertation is exclusively dedicated to the study of fictional hypertexts which all share the characteristic of being interpretative as well as explorative, this function will not be included in our model.

The author's own analysis, which is based on the statistical method of correspondence analysis, shows that works being published in print and those which rely on the electronic environment - when classified according to the categories quoted above - largely overlap rather than being on the completely opposite side of the scale. Although in this presentation I do not aim to replicate the analysis used by AARSETH, I will nevertheless use the suggested categories in order to more closely describe the primary texts in question.

4. Technology

> Imagine if Shakespeare had had to invent the mechanism of acting and staging dynamics in his spare time in order to conceptualize King Lear as a play? [56]

A number of early hypertext scholars have overemphasised the importance of techno-logical advancement for hypertextual writing - "[I]n these analyses, technical innovation is presented as a cause of social improvement and political and intellectual liberation, a historical move away from the old repressive media."[18, p.14]. While it is true that indeed the electronic medium opens up a whole new range of possibilities for literature, this is nevertheless only a limited view, leaving other considerations aside. Of course it can be argued that with no other type of literature, the text is as closely tied to the medium as here, but surely it is still not the only characteristic of hypertext.

A work of hyperfiction is presented in a medium that itself is comparatively new, and since the internet as a publishing-environment influences the kind of writing that is being produced in a very obvious way, it is advisable to include a closer look at the technical aspects of these works. Without having in mind to go into too much detail here, I find it necessary to point out which tools ('authoring-tools') writers for example have at their disposal in order to create their hypertexts, and to make some statements regarding the way in which these programmed structures are read - or rather used - by the audience. Developing his concept of "critical hyperreading", BURBULES [27, p.118] stresses the importance of "looking behind the scenes" of hypertext production in order to understand it:

4. Technology

Just as specialists in other fields [...] can be the sharpest critics of other practitio-
ners because they know the conventions, tricks, and moves that establish a sense of
style [...] so also should hyperreaders [...] know what goes into selecting material
for a page, making links, organising a cluster of separate pages into a hyperlinked
Web site, and so forth.

4.1. The Interface

One problem which concerns the production as well as the reading process of hyperfiction is the fact that the internet can be browsed with a variety of browsers and
screen-resolutions. Most authors are quite aware of this and usually give the preferred
browser-type at the beginning of their work in order to ensure proper access for readers
intending to read the respective work. Hence, depending on the preferred use of browser-
programmes such as *Microsoft Internet Explorer, Netscape Navigator, Mozilla, Firefox*
or *Opera*, the work can be presented on the respective reader's screen quite differently.
In other words, the author is not able to predict entirely what his work will look like.

A browser-programme offers a variety of conventionalised functions supporting the
user to be able to access the internet as easily and effectively as possible. These functions
also offer an interesting view on hyperfictional works. For instance, the 'home'-button
which takes the reader back to a predetermined start-address as well as the collection of
'bookmarks' or 'favourites' are always visible to the user and thus 'only one click away'.
In other words, when following the reading-path of a piece of hyperfiction, it is as easy to
click a link belonging to this work as it is possible to choose one of the links the browser-
interface constantly shows. Hence, this interface makes the user constantly aware of the
fact that he can follow a narrative or check the latest world-news for instance. Here,
we can establish obvious connections to the characteristic of intertextuality mentioned
before in Chapter 3.5.

Furthermore, the browser records the sequence of visited websites in its 'history', enabling the user to reconstruct exactly which addresses he has visited and move backward and forward through this sequence with the respective browser-buttons. This technical detail refers to the fact that despite a hypertext's fragmentation, the reading of it - seen on a temporal axis - occurs in a linear fashion, thus qualifying the notion of linearity. Also, these back-and-forward buttons are an important navigational tool, as will be shown in the analysis of **** *[four stars]* [20] later on.

Finally, every browser offers the possibility for the reader to "look behind the scenes" of a hypertext by providing the source-code of the respective pages. This is especially helpful when trying to analyse the internal link-structures of hyperfictional works.

4.2. Platforms

There is a wide range of platforms, i.e. software and so-called plug-ins that are used to create hyperfiction on the internet. These are for example the well-known standard-language of the internet, namely HTML *(Hypertext Markup Language)* used to determine the arrangement of the work's components on screen as well as the design of the written text, special scripting-languages enabling the programmer to integrate additional functions to his work, such as *Javascript*, and multi-media extensions adding features such as video and highly complex animation, like *Shockwave* or *Flash*. Depending on the author's knowledge of internet programming and the software tools available to him, the work can be produced in a number of ways.

When computer technology was still in its early years, only experienced programmers could write applications and thus communicate with the machines and make them respond in the special and desired way. Today, the programs available for the building of internet-based works ('authoring tools') are manifold, and on the web there are so many voluntary help forums and communities that it requires little effort to become accustomed to these tools and start writing.

What is also important to note here is the fact that, either intentionally or unintentionally, by using the respective technology, the author can both include and exclude certain audiences. As many webmasters will agree, there is not one fixed standard that enables one to fully predict what a certain website will look like. There are in fact numerous operating systems, browser versions and screen resolutions to consider. Thus, the author, apart from the fact that he leaves the freedom to the reader to make use of the hypertext's interlinking and explore it at will, loses a certain amount of control because of this uncertainty.

4.3. The Icon

The icon is an integral part of a work of hyperfiction which not only relies on written text (i.e. graphical representations of the sounds of a language) in order to transfer meaning. It is defined[1] as "[...] an image, picture, representation, etc. [...]" and "[...] a symbol resembling or analogous to the thing it represents [...]" and thus used in quite a general way. Although the term "icon" originated in the world of printed publications, in quite a modern sense the term carries an extra-meaning: "[...] a pictorial representation of a facility available on a computer system, that enables the facility to be activated by means of a screen cursor rather than by a textual instruction [...]".

The use of icons in the latter sense was developed by the computer-company APPLE MACINTOSH. Initially, the aim of the system-engineers was to build a user-interface that could be interacted with by means of clicking small symbols on the so-called 'desktop'. Thus, interaction became intuitive, and a lot of these icons became standardised. Later on, the concept was worked into MICROSOFT's *Windows* operating system and was distributed world-wide. Today, modern interface design, i.e. design for websites, has to acknowledge these standards and uses them accordingly. A little image of an envelope for example depicts an email-link, a symbolic house indicates a link that forwards the user to the index- (home-) page. While these small navigational elements are primarily used in connection with non-fictional texts, i.e. internet news-sites and search-engines,

---

[1] `http://www.wordreference.com/definition/icon.htm`, accessed 25.04.05

they are also used in an artistic background and thus carry literary meaning as well. We we will see in the analysis of the corpus how successful the individual artists employ these icons to obtain the desired artistic effect.

4.4. The Code

In hypertext there is a hidden layer of information underneath the textual surface that presents itself to the reader.

When we take for example a highly complex and rhizomatic work of hyperfiction, it is imaginable that there are textual fragments which do not appear to the reader at all, because he has chosen a path which does not involve this particular fragment, or has stopped his reading at a stage where it was impossible for him to encounter this fragment. Referring to what INTEMANN [46, pp.92-93] suggests, these fragments that only potentially exist but are not actively inserted into the reader's reading, do not belong to the text since they are not relevant for this specific instance of communication. In other words, they can become relevant for example in another reading of the same work, but for this specific instance, they do not belong to the text. A second implication is surely the relationship between the ground- and the surface-structure of hypertexts. What the reader can see on screen and what the author has written for the internet-browser to interpret can vary significantly. However, unless the ground-structure is not explicitly offered to the reader on screen (as in so-called 'codework'), it does not belong to the text as such.

In technical terms, the ground-structure is the programming-language and hence the basis for the works of hyperfiction we encounter on the internet. In a previous chapter, DAHLSTRÖM has also referred to this phenomenon as mark-up (cf. Chapter 3): Specialised tags that help the software, typically a browser, to interpret what is stored on the server and make it accessible for the human readership.

> [...] Even in the case of a simple web page, we are faced with a divorce of the unified document into at least two [...] or three textual layers. Each of these is editable at minimal level: the binary level of ones and zeros, the syntactic layer of

marked up text along with its markup tags, and finally the presentational layer of a displayed text at the temporary screen or at a fixed, laser printed page.[...]

There are a number of writers using the artistic potential of this code, which results in works usually referred to as 'codework'. John CALEY [28, p.1] gives the following definition:

> Potentially codework is a term for literature which uses, addresses, and incorporates code: as underlying language-animating or language-generating programming, as a special type of language in itself, or as an intrinsic part of the new surface language or 'interface text', as I call it, of writing in networked and programmable media.

Referring to the individual works codework-artists produce, he suggests:

> In particular, the address of this type of intermixed, contaminated language is often concerned - as show in the work of all these writers - with issues of identity, gender, subjectivity, technology, technoscience, and the mutating and mutable influence they bring to bear on human lives and on human-human and human-machine relationships.

Later on in his essay, CALEY refers to one of his own codeworks:

```
on write
  repeat twice
    do "global" & characteristics
  end repeat
  repeat with programmers = one to always
    if touching then
      put essential into invariance
    else
      put the round of simplicity + engineering / synchronicity + one into
  invariance
  end write
```

Here, we are presented with a mixture of what could best be described as an extract of programming code, containing strictly logical and mathematical prompts on the one hand, and natural language on the other.

In order to conclude this overview, I would like to give an example of so-called 'ASCII-art'[2], which tries to produce drawings by means of positioning computer-symbols in a special way. In this respect, they can also be referred to code-work in the widest sense.

Figure 4.1.

Garfield in ASCII-art

[2]`http://www.chris.com/ascii/`, accessed 25.04.05

5. Hypertext and Narrative

> [...] Plot, characterization, and setting, in my view, are as important in a work of hypertext fiction as they are in any other kind of fiction. What differs is how these elements are developed, and what function they serve in the story. In our case, we went with a picaresque, on-the-road narrative.[1]

The central analytical methods for the detailed analysis of hypertext will be provided by narratology: Here, I would like to focus on the features of this area of literary studies which can be fruitfully applied to works of hyperfiction. Also in this chapter, I will try to prove the validity of these categories by giving some short examples in order to support my findings.

Interdisciplinary narratology   In Chapter 3 I have already discussed the prominent features of hypertexts as they are perceived by theorists and authors. The aim of the present chapter now is to integrate concepts such as non-linearity, intertextuality, and interactivity with categories of narrative analysis in order to form an analytical matrix. For this work, I would like the term 'narratology' to be understood in a very broad and interdisciplinary sense. According to ONEGA/LANDA, "[n]arratology now appears to be reverting to its etymological sense, a multi-disciplinary study of narrative which negotiates and incorporates the insights of many other critical discourses that involve narrative forms of representation."[67, p.1] For their purposes, they formulate both a narrow and a rather broad definition of narrative. With regard to hypertexts and the more complex theoretical issues which they trigger, I have opted for the broad definition

---

[1]http://www.unknownhypertext.com/owlhypertext.htm, 25.04.05

in order to be able to account for the many different existing variations of hyperfiction on the internet:

> A narrative is the semiotic representation of a series of events meaningfully connected in a temporal and causal way. Films, plays, comic strips, novels, newsreels, diaries, chronicles and treatises of geological history are all narratives in this wider sense. Narratives can therefore be constructed using an ample variety of semiotic media: written or spoken language, visual images, gestures and acting, as well as a combination of these. [67, p.3]

This definition, although not explicitly mentioning hypertexts, nevertheless provides us with some good starting-points for our further discussion. To begin with, let us consider the expression "meaningfully connected in a temporal and causal way": What is being referred to here obviously is the main constituent of every narrative ARISTOTLE already centered his *Poetics* around: the plot. The question that needs to be investigated is, to what extent can we talk about plot with regard to hypertexts? As has been mentioned in the chapter on coherence (cf. Chapter 3.7), it seems problematic to develop a series of events when the individual constituents of the plot can be read in random order. Other questions are: Is it possible for the author of a hypertext to make sure that the individual lexias of his work are connected meaningfully? Especially with regard to highly complex, rhizomatic works, the controlled development of a plot seems more than questionable. Of course, we could also question the term "meaningfully" itself. In the widest possible sense, even such a text outlined above can have its meaning, although it might not be universally accepted by the majority of the readers. The question of readership and individual readings is, in this respect, particularly interesting, since I would suggest that with no other genre in literature can there be so many divergent readings of one and the same text. This makes it of course even harder to trace unique storylines.

Furthermore, another interesting point of departure which the definition cited above establishes is the "series of events": Once again, ONEGA/LANDA refer to the plot and try to investigate what makes up a narrative and how this can be analysed:

> The very definition of narrative we propose [...] assumes that narratives are com-
> posite entities in a number of senses, that a narrative can be analysed into the
> events that compose it, and that these events can be studied according to the
> position with respect to each other.

Here, the authors describe the succession of events. Yet again, what is taken for
granted with respect to linear fiction the authors are referring to, has to be questioned
in view of the new textual and organisational possibilities of internet-authors. Although
certainly a hypertext is indeed made of individual modules and thus represents a 'com-
posite entity', the question of how they relate to each other, i.e. what their position
is on the syntagmatic level of analysis is much harder to answer. Therefore, we need
to have a closer look at individual works of hyperfiction in order to find out how this
definition can be applied to the new texts. Another issue the definition above touches is
the use of different media. Although the internet or hypertext are not explicitly listed
here, one could very well imagine that these also fit in the context the writers had in
mind originally.

In the same vein, NÜNNING/NÜNNING argue in favour of a narratology which should
be "transgenerisch", "intermedial", and "interdisziplinär" in their opinion:

> Geht man [...] von einem weiten Begriff von Narrativität aus und beschränkt man
> sich auf das Merkmal der erzählten Handlung, so zeigt sich, daß auch vermeintlich
> nicht-narrative Genres wie Comics, Filme und Dramen sehr wohl eine Geschichte
> 'erzählen'. [66, p.7]

With regard to hypertext, the article *"Cyberage-Narratologie: Erzähltheorie und Hyperfiktion"* by Klaudia SEIBEL [76] is also very instructive: the author sheds some light
on the new issues that are being raised by the innovative electronic texts that are currently developing. Beside others, an interesting question she raises is whether narrativity
and interactivity - the latter being one of the prominent features of hypertext and having

been discussed before in Chapter 3.3 - can coexist at all. Referring to the immersion into a story, she also alludes to the problem that the hypertext constantly refers back to itself, i.e. the reader/user can never really "lose" himself into the story. Rather, he constantly has to make choices as to how the plot should continue. SEIBEL also refers to electronic texts with a higher immersive potential - interactive computer games - which allow a higher degree of user participation and interactivity.

Having thus prepared the theoretical ground for our discussion, I now would like to consider scholars such as BAL, RIMMON-KENAN, CHATMAN, and the recent publications of NÜNNING/NÜNNING for a more detailed analysis. I will also refer to a narratological model developed by WENZEL particularly with regard to the dichotomy between story- and discourse-levels of analysis. Proceeding from a comprehensive model for text analysis, I will use the narratological categories developed by these scholars as a basis for examining the works in question. In the course of this chapter, I will try to summarise the most important aspects of this analytical model and at the same time try to open it up for use with the 'new' texts this dissertation is dealing with.

It has to be noted at this point that the purpose of the following paragraphs is not to set up an entirely new model for narrative analysis. Rather, I would like to broadly outline which analytical categories are at hand and - more importantly - which of these could be fruitfully used in connection with the analysis of hypertextual fiction.

Inter- vs. intrafragmental levels of analysis Hypertexts consists of a number of fragments/modules interconnected by links. These individual fragments can be single words, in most cases, however, they contain one or more sentences. Hence, for a literary analysis of hypertexts we will have to arrange our discussion on two different levels, namely on the intrafragmental level, i.e. that of the structure *within* individual constituents, and the interfragmental level, which describes the interrelationship *between* the individual fragments. As we have seen, as far as the plot of a story is concerned, it is created by a succession of events. Here, we need to ask whether every fragment contains an event or whether the subdivision of fragments follows other rules.

5.1. Story

Looking at the story-level of narrative texts, theorists usually make the differentiation between 'events' and 'existents': the former refers both to 'actions' and 'happenings' in the plotline of the given story, the latter describe both 'characters' and the 'setting'.

5.1.1. Events

In *The Unknown* for example, the individual fragments are usually made up of at least five to ten sentences, so in a way, each fragment can be seen as an independent and coherent whole able to carry elements of the story. The hypertext itself resembles a travel report with individual episodes describing the events of the authors' booktour. In a fragment named "What Is To Be Done is What We Are Discussing", we find a series of events on an the intrafragmental level:

> Dirk has stood up somewhat unsteadily to put another record on and this time it is Billie Holiday, a bird in a golden cage. William has seen Scott looking at Marla and he is trying to put together this terrible jigsaw puzzle, this childs game, with his numb and yellowed fingertips. For awhile [sic] there is the issue of cigarettes and as Frank passes around a pack of Gauloises we are relieved of that terrible uncomfortableness that is all a part of not-knowing. And then there is a silence as we are swept toward the center of the record where everything is named. And then there is the crackle of the needle in its last dance into the end of the spiral and then only Dirk: "Do records spin the other way in the northern hemisphere?"[2]

Reading this fragment without having any background information about the whole work, the reader does not know any of the characters of course. But the short episode shows the trace of a (trivial) plot, namely the putting on of a record and the reaction of the characters who seem to be drunk.

---

[2]`http://www.unknownhypertext.com/cortazar.htm`, accessed 25.04.2005

5.1.2. Existents

5.1.2.1. Setting

As far as the setting of a story is concerned, WENZEL illustrates the fact that especially oppositions of locations can be connected to social, historical, and political concepts contextualising narratives:

> So finden wir räumliche Oppositionen vor wie 'oben und unten', 'hoch und niedrig',
> 'rechts und links', 'nah und fern' sowie - auf einer konkreten Ebene - 'Haus und
> Stadt', 'Haus und Wald', 'Stadt und Land' oder 'Heimat und Fremde'. [89, pp.179-
> 180]

With reference to *These Waves of Girls* [7], which will be analysed later on, we can establish the binary opposition of Tracey's recollections of tranquil and beautiful nature, and what happens to her in the city. Regarding *The Unknown* [9], a typical description of a city authors come to is:

> Cincinnati. The name speaks of modern gothic architecture rearing up on hills
> built on mounds of the bones of Native Americans. Her taxis weave through the
> citys nightlife, her charm and sparkle. She is a city with a firm handshake but bad
> eye contact. Seven hills. Flying pigs. Grease and laughter and pockets everywhere.
> Pockets too deep for the mind to process. Of time and division.[3] [...]

This example shows - and there are many more similar fragments in *The Unknown* - how the setting is described in this special case. Interestingly, this setting plays a role both on the inter- and the intrafragmental levels: with regard to the former, after having browsed through the piece of hyperfiction for some time we recognise that the description of Cincinnati adds to the overall plot, namely the authors' booktour through the States. However, within the fragment, the setting is also suitably described and does not need the other fragments in order for the reader to make sense of it.

---

[3]`http://www.unknownhypertext.com/brochure.htm`, accessed 25.04.05

Quite often in secondary literature on the subject the reception of hypertext, it is compared to the traversal of a physical space.[4] As in a labyrinth, the reader has to make his way through the text, passing different forking paths, i.e. text-fragments asking for a direction to take, on the way.[5]

5.1.2.2. Characters & Characterisation

Characters of a story perform various tasks, can be identified by certain traits, and can be presented in many ways. We often find stereotypical characters such as protagonist/antagonist, helpers, witnesses or even the moral judgement between good and evil characters. Also, as WENZEL suggests, it is often complicated to separate the characters from the events, because "[...] Figuren haben oftmals keine andere Aufgabe, als bestimmte Funktionen für die Handlung zu erfüllen [...]" [89, p.178]

In order to be able to make more precise statements about characters, RIMMON-KENAN quoting EWEN[6] suggests classifying them by their complexity, their development and the degree of penetration into their 'inner life':

> At one pole on the axis of *complexity* he locates characters constructed around a single trait or around one dominant trait along with a few secondary ones. Allegorical figures, caricatures, and types belong to this pole. In the first, the proper name represents the single trait around which the character is constructed (Pride, Sin). In the second, one out of the various qualities is exaggerated and made prominent [...]. And in the third, the prominent trait is grasped as representative of a whole group rather than as a purely individual quality [...][70, p.41]

Characters can thus be classified as one-dimensional or multi-dimensional, depending on which role the author would like the respective character to perform in the narrative. Usually, the main characters such as the protagonist and the antagonist tend to be

---

[4]Quite fittingly, BOLTER titled his theoretical treatise *Writing Space* [24].

[5]Cf. Chapter 3.3

[6]J. EWEN, The theory of character in narrative fiction, *Hasifrut*, 3, 1-30, 1971; *Character in Narrative*, 1980

multi-dimensional, while their friends and helpers often stay one-dimensional, because they serve only one purpose or have only one characteristic trait.

In connection with the dimensionality of characters, another important aspect is whether they are static or developing. Broadly we can state that the main actors of the plot undergo a certain development, and their emotional or social stance is altered at the end when compared to that of the beginning. In contrast, static characters remain unchanged and unaffected by the events surrounding them.

> The third axis, penetration into the 'inner life' ranges from characters like [...] whose consciousness is presented from within, to the likes of [...] seen only from the outside, their minds remaining opaque. [70, p.42]

When the reader is enabled to look deep into the mind or the emotional situation of a character, then the level of penetration is quite high. This is for example true, when SHAKESPEARE makes his characters soliloquise, so that the audience becomes acquainted with what the protagonist or antagonist of the story is living through. Similarly, descriptions of characters are developed by authors of hyperfiction. In *These Waves of Girls*, for example, the author describes her friend Vanessa:

> At six she had an attractive, wandering hazel eye. I would brush the hair off her face, her earnest hands trying to stop me. With Vanessa things happened. All sorts of lessons that left metal tastes in my mouth. In our mouths as we kissed. She was born in Canada, England on her lips, her accent strong against my tongue. We went to different schools. Her friends were not my friends. And there was need, in her hunting pack, to keep pace.[7]

The description of the character of Vanessa rests on this particular fragment, and there is no immanent need for the reader to follow a link in order to create a coherent reading.

---

[7]`http://www.yorku.ca/caitlin/waves/vanessa.htm`, accessed 25.04.05

It needs to be said at this stage that especially *The Unknown* is a rather atypical example in that it very much resembles a printed publication. The individual fragments are long enough for intrafragmental coherence to be established, and as far as narratological categories on story-level are concerned, these do not have to be specifically altered in order to account for hyperfiction.

There are other texts that make it much more difficult to find starting-points for analysis. In *My Boyfriend came back from the War*, the initial lexia only consists of two sentences: "My boyfriend came back from the war. After dinner they left us alone." In this case, both sentences initiate a series of expectations on the part of the reader, and thus form an ideal starting-point for this narrative. However, on the intrafragmental level, the reader receives only traces of information with regard to the story. Hence, in this case the focus necessarily needs to shift to the interfragmental level in order to find points of reference for the analysis of the present narrative. When the reader clicks on the sentence, the text unfolds successively, revealing the dialogue between the man and the woman, which I will refer to in more detail in Chapter 6.4. For the moment it suffices to say that this instance is a typical example of a text that relies on interfragmental relationships in order to build coherence: Fragments such as "Where are you? I can't see you" and "he was my neighbor" only contribute to a coherent reading when seen in relation to each other. This necessity is also enhanced by the fact that some of the fragments appear on the screen simultaneously since the author makes use of 'frames' (cf. Chapter 4).

As a preliminary summary it can be said that with regard to the constituents of the story-level of analysis, there is a continuum between texts the fragments of which establish coherence on an intrafragmental level, i.e. texts that closely resemble their printed counterparts, and texts which consist of very small fragments that need other neighboring fragments for meaning to be established. The story-level of analysis does not really pose a challenge to the existing categories of narratological analysis. Although the individual elements are potentially spread across many different fragments, they are nevertheless present in the same way they are in traditional printed literature.

5.2. Discourse

More innovative and interesting results, therefore, are to be expected from the examination of the discourse-level of analysis. Here, as CHATMAN [32, pp.63ff] proposes with reference to GENETTE[8], especially 'order', 'duration', and 'frequency' deserve closer inspection, since they correlate with crucial characteristics of hypertext, such as non-linearity for instance.

5.2.1. Order

Nonlinearity has been identified as one of the most important characteristics of hypertext, which has also been discussed in detail in Chapter 3.1. We have seen with reference to STORRER's understanding of linearity, how important it is to differentiate between the medium the text is presented in ('mediale Linearität') and the abstract textual concept of linearity ('konzeptionelle Linearität'). Furthermore, the concept of linearity can also be analysed on the intra- and interfragmental level: In hyperfictional narratives, the individual lexias consist of a number of sentences the sequence of which is impossible to change. Thus, on the intrafragmental level, we often find a degree of narrative linearity that is comparable to that of traditional printed literature. It is only when the single fragments become short and highly interconnected in a given work that the interfragmental level becomes more relevant.

Finally, it is important to refer to both the causal as well as the temporal structure of the successive lexias.[9] As regards the latter, a differentiation needs to be established between cases where story and discourse have the same order, and cases of 'achrony': Here, by either interrupting the order by 'analepsis' ('flashback'), i.e. the discursive reference

---

[8]GENETTE, G., "Time and Narrative in *A la recherche du temps perdu*," trans. Paul de Man, in J. Hillis Miller, ed., *Aspects of Narrative* (New York, 1970), pp. 93-118

[9]In this respect, links function as the basic structuring-principle of hypertexts, as has been referred to in detail in Chapter 3.2.4.

to events which have happened in the past, and 'prolepsis' ('flashforward') depicting an event that will occur in the future.

A question which needs to lead our analysis of the body of primary texts, then, could be, whether different structural types of hypertexts (cf. SUTER's typology) predetermine a certain order of discourse. It can be guessed that tree- and labyrinthine structures lead to a more sequential build-up of the plot, since the interfragmental connections are weaker and therefore less random.

5.2.2. Duration

How long does it take for the narrator to present the story to the reader, and what is the relationship between discourse-time and story-time? In a work of hyperfiction, as has been already been referred to in Chapter 3.6 on the open text, it is often the case that the borders delineating the respective work are sometimes difficult to establish. Often, texts overlap with others, or, because of their very structure, do not 'end' at all but provide a sheer infinite textual space the reader can move around in at will - until he 'has enough'. It is also possible to encounter one specific fragment more than once, which - apart from implications concerning the plot - also modifies the duration of the discourse. In other words, especially in highly complex structures such as rhizomes and multiple-rhizomes, the investigation of duration requires a modified view on the temporal development of hypertextual narratives.

The classical subdivision of the aspect of duration is given by CHATMAN [32, pp.67-68]:

(1) summary: discourse-time is shorter than story-time; (2) ellipsis: the same as (1), except that discourse-time is zero; (3) scene: discourse-time and story-time are equal; (4) stretch: the discourse-time is longer than story-time; (5) pause: the same as (4), except that story-time is zero.

The occurrence of these categories, which will be included in our analytical model, will also be questioned and examined with regard to the corpus of primary texts in the final chapter of this dissertation.

5.2.3. Frequency

In case the narrator chooses to repeat a specific part of the story, we talk about 'frequency'. JAHN [48] offers the following categorisation:

- **singulative telling** Recounting once what happened once.
- **repetitive telling** Recounting several times what happened once.
- **iterative telling** Recounting once what happened n times.

With regard to the three frequential modes outlined above, we are in a position to establish parallels between the latter and the different structural types of hypertexts. For instance, works of hyperfiction which are organised in a comparatively linear fashion, the reader will prevailingly encounter 'singulative telling' in that he is very likely to access a specific lexia containing an event only once. In contrast, hypertexts which follow the organisational principle of the rhizome, i.e. which are interlinked to a very high degree, are also quite likely to be characterised by repetitive telling, since a fragment can be visited more than once and thus the same event is told several times.

5.2.4. Narrative Situation & Focalisation

The specific point of view from which the story is told, i.e. the narrative situation is also of great interest in the analysis of narrative texts. Here, a differentiation is usually made between the one who *sees* (=focaliser) and the one who *tells* (narrator). Regarding the former, we distinguish between 'external' and 'internal' focalisation, depending on the point of view:

> A text is anchored on a focalizer's point of view when it presents (and does not transcend) the focalizer's thoughts, reflections and knowledge, his/her actual and imaginary perceptions, as well as his/her cultural and ideological orientation. [48]

A 'heterodiegetic' narrator (i.e. an "Er"-Erzähler in the terminology originally developed by STANZEL) does not belong to the 'storyworld' [59]. In contrast, the 'homodiegetic narrator' (i.e. "Ich"-Erzähler, with the differentiation between 'narrating-I' or 'experiencing-I') is a part of the internal structure of the story, i.e. he belongs to the cast of characters. As far as the narrative situation is concerned, JAHN [48] enumerates the following possibilities:

- A **first-person narrative** is told by a narrator who is present as a character in his/her story; it is a story of events s/he has experienced him- or herself, a story of personal experience. The individual who acts as a narrator (narrating I) is also a character (experiencing I) on the level of action [...]

- An **authorial narrative** is told by a narrator who is absent from the story, i.e., does not appear as a character in the story. The authorial narrator tells a story involving other people. An authorial narrator sees the story from an outsider's position, often a position of absolute authority that allows her/him to know everything about the story's world and its characters [...]

- A **figural narrative** presents a story as if seeing it through the eyes of a character [...]

Very frequently in hypertextual fiction, the narrator takes a position completely outside his story, reflecting on the work itself, thus introducing *metafictional* elements. In almost all of the pieces we are going to analyse, the author(s) deliver a theoretical foundation for their works, or explicit instructions as to how the respective text is meant to be read. In *The Ballad of Sand and Harry Soot* by Stephanie STRICKLAND [16] it says in a fragment one can reach by clicking "How?":

How to Read the Ballad

There are three navigation methods through The Ballad of Sand and Harry Soot, and the reader may combine them in any fashion. They are:

- the Random reading
- the Complete reading

- the Link-Driven reading.[10]

The lack of metafictional elements is actually an exception to the rule. With regard to *kokura* (discussion in Chapter 6.5), Michael SHUMATE [78] remarks quite fittingly:

> One important thing *not* found in "Kokura" is any discussion of hypertext. No wondering how it is or is not like life, print literature, film, or anything else. It is not mentioned or acknowledged in any way, in the text, prologue, or credits. Any time this is absent from a hypertext I am profoundly grateful–I take it as a sign that the field is maturing and that its practitioners are ceasing to fret about it so much. There are other topics to turn these wonderful tools upon, and Arnold and Denby take up the challenge without looking over their shoulders at print, critics, postmodernism, or anything else other than their subject. *(my emphasis)*

5.2.5. Mode

The events as well as the characters of the story can, broadly speaking, be presented either in showing or telling mode. We talk about the former mode in connection with a narration that relates all the events without much mediation or reflection. In other words, the reader takes the position of an eye-witness looking at the actions of the characters and all the events in the story. In contrast, in the latter, the characters are minutely described, i.e. they are characterised by the narrator rather than by their actions. The most straightforward method, therefore, is termed 'direct definition' and usually means that the authorial narrator explicitly describes and thus defines a character; in other words, this mode of presentation is the 'telling mode'. In contrast, as RIMMON-KENAN suggests, the characters can also be presented using the 'showing mode': "[...] character is a construct, put together by the reader from various indications dispersed throughout the text." [70, p.36]

---

[10]http://www.wordcircuits.com/gallery/sandsoot/how.html, accessed 25.04.05

5.2.6. Style

Finally, regarding the discourse level of analysis, the use of different styles also contributes to the overall aesthetic effect of the work. Usually, we define the 'direct style', the 'free indirect style', and the 'indirect style'. According to JAHN [48], direct style or discourse features a "[...] direct quotation of a character's speech ('direct speech') or (verbalized) thought ('direct thought') [...]", thus if a statement is put in quotation marks, we can almost be sure that we are dealing with the direct style. The following short extract from *The Unknown*[11] is a good example for direct discourse:

> Exhausted by their labors, combined with that peculiar adrenaline letdown that always accompanied doing hypertext live, the Unknown collapsed on a large couch in the corner.
>
> I'll never do that again, William gasped. Its hard acting like I have an independent sense of volition.
>
> I second that motion, Scott panted. That fucking camel nearly killed me. Fuckin' drenched in camel slobber.

Free indirect style or discourse is defined by JAHN [48] like this:

> [...] A representation of a character's words ('free indirect speech') or verbalized thoughts ('free indirect thought') which is (a) 'indirect' in the sense that pronouns and tenses of the quoted discourse are aligned with the pronoun/tense structure of the current narrative situation, and (b) 'free' to the extent that the discourse quoted appears in the form of a non-subordinate clause. [...]

Finally, JAHN [48] suggests the following definition for 'indirect style':

> [...] A form of representing a character's words ('indirect speech') or (verbalized) thoughts ('indirect thought') which uses a reporting clause of introductory attributive discourse, places the discourse quoted in a subordinate clause bound to the deictic orientation of the narrator, and generally summarizes, interprets, and grammatically straightens the character's language.

---

[11]`http://www.unknownhypertext.com/hard_code15.htm`, accessed 25.04.05

5. Hypertext and Narrative

Having thus given a broad overview of the categories of narratological analysis as well as their various implications, we are now in a position to analyse the text-corpus against this theoretical background. What is of special interest here is to find out how the characteristics of hypertext "interact" with the narratological categories and offer new insights into the structure of narratives.

6. Analysis

6.1. The Model

Before applying the categories which have been extracted and discussed in the previous chapters, I have set up a preliminary model, which - it has to be noted, however - is not meant to be exclusive or exhaustive. Points which could be further elaborated and worked into a completely new model are for example the social and political implications which play a role with specific regards to hypertexts: Seeing the internet as a world-wide phenomenon where geographical (and connected to this, cultural) separations which have been taken for granted no longer apply, it is certain that this is also mirrored in the fiction distributed via the internet. Furthermore, even if the new medium is claimed to be quite a democratic medium, access to it is doubtless restricted, and generally speaking - apart from Australia and New Zealand - only the northern hemisphere benefits from this technology. In developing countries as well as totalitarian regimes accessing the internet is often not possible. Also, the role of film, comics, and visual arts and their theoretical foundation would have fitted into the model but need to be referred to elsewhere.

I also acknowledge the fact that the model suggests clear-cut and separate categories where in reality there are of course overlaps and interdependencies. For instance, one of the major characteristics of hypertext discussed earlier on - interactivity - is closely related to the concept of 'transiency' developed by AARSETH in that a high degree of user-interaction automatically demands an intransient text. As a result, I will not work down a check-list within my analyses, referring to each category individually, but rather discuss the various categories according to the way they work together in the respective work. Still, as a means to summarise the crucial theoretical approaches and to serve as a guiding line in the ensuing analyses I believe it nevertheless to be a valid and justified approach to construct the following matrix:

HYPERTEXTUAL CHARACTERISTICS	
technology	interface, platform, icon, code
navigation	structure overviews, global/local context cues
links	link vs. link-target, navigation, rhetorical properties
crossmediality	sound/text & image/text-relationships, film
interactivity	degree of user participation
linearity	*un-/mono-/mehrfachsequenziert*
intertextuality	general, special
production	instability, referencing
reception	closure, coherence
open text	text boundaries
TYPOLOGY I: AARSETH	
Determinability	Determinable, indeterminable
Transiency	Transient, intransient
Access	Random, controlled
Linking	Explicit, conditional, none

Table 6.1.

Compound Model (1)

TYPOLOGY II: SUTER	
Hypertextual structure	axial(linear), tentacle, tree-structure, maze, net/rhizome, multiple rhizome

HYPERTEXT AS NARRATIVE	
Story	
events (actions/happenings)	temporal + causal arrangement
characters/characterisation	static/developing, one-dimensional/multi-dimensional
setting	place, atmosphere
Discourse	
order	normal sequence, achrony (analepsis/prolepsis), linearity
duration	summary, ellipsis/omission, scene, stretch, pause
frequency	singulative/repetitive/iterative telling
narrator/focalisor	external/internal, homodiegetic/heterodiegetic, (first-person/authorial/figural), metafiction
mode	direct speech, summary
	direct/telling, indirect/showing
style	language/register

Table 6.2.

Compound Model (2)

6.2. The Unknown

⇒ Author(s):   William GILLESPIE, Scott RETTBERG, Dirk STRATTON,

　　　　　　　　　Frank MARQUARD

⇒ Award: trAce/Alt-X Hypertext Competition 1998 1st Prize

⇒ ELO category: Hypertext fiction, Recorded Readings/Performances of Fiction

General description and technology　This work is one of the best-known pieces of hy-perfiction on the internet. It has been awarded 1st prize together with GENIWATE's *Rice* in the *trAce/Alt-X Hypertext Competition* 1998, and its main characteristic is the fact that it can be described as road-movie meta-hypertext. The four authors travel through the United States and give live readings of their hypertext. Events accompanying these readings are written down or recorded on tape and later incorporated into the existing body of fragments which make up *The Unknown*. I have chosen this primary work for a number of reason: Firstly, I would like to highlight the idea of "meta-hypertext" and at the same time give an example of how fictional narrative and theoretical considerations as well as critical self-reflexivity can meet in one work.

Also, as has been already suggested in Chapter 5, this work shows the degree to which traditional printed literature and hypertexts are interrelated in that the individual modules of *The Unknown* form self-contained entities which can be analysed as one would do with short printed fiction. Moreover, the work is also quite interesting with respect to the genre it belongs to, namely the travelogue: By means of combining various texts, sound-bites, postcards, and photographs, the authors describe the movement through the country and through time and thus form their work out of fragments, which indeed makes a fragmented hypertext the obvious publication-method. Here, I propose that this way of narrating events is especially suited for this genre, and it is possible to yet again establish strong connections between the printed and the electronic world of writing. This is especially true because the motif of *The Unknown* is actually a reading-tour through bookshops. The authors centre their individual pieces of writing around their fictional printed book (*The Unknown Anthology*) which they promote. The hypertext itself, therefore, as a whole tells the story of these authors and their way of marketing the novel they are actually writing 'on the go'.

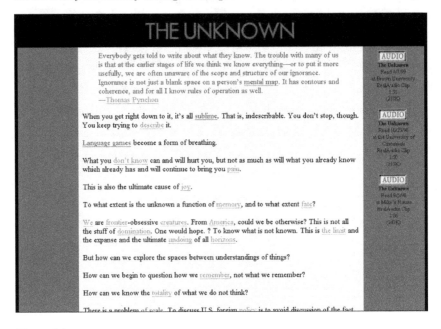

Figure 6.1.

"The Unknown"

The work does not involve elaborate multi-medial items, such as *Flash*-animations or the like, but rather relies on standard *HTML*-programming and simple graphics. Thus, the narrative is accessible by a wide range of (older) computer-systems and slower connections in that it does not require additional software in turn requiring additional connection-bandwidth and processing-speed.

Navigation and linking When the reader enters the hypertext, the first thing he sees is the title of the work which is located on top of an introductory image. When this page is reloaded several times, the image actually emerges as a randomly chosen file that is different every time, for example depicting a tombstone with "The Unknown" written onto it, or the authors themselves. From the outset, the introductory image embodies what the work is dealing with: it is indeed unknown what the beginning will be like and what the initial mood is going to be. This randomness - which is a tool also successfully used by other producers of hypertexts - allows the author to create divergent readings without him or the reader changing or deciding anything at all. Behind the scenes the individual fragments - in the present case various photographs - are reshuffled every time the page is loaded. As a result, given that there is only one image visible at a time, but potentially innumerable images the small shuffling-script chooses from exist, there is quite an obvious difference between the background- and the surface-structure.

At this point it is also quite revealing to reconsider what we have mentioned earlier on about the function of the author: randomness is a very strong tool to undermine the writer's controlling function over his own text. While with links, he has at least a limited amount of control, now the outcome of the work is completely unpredictable.

On clicking the randomly created image, the reader accesses the starting page of the hypertext, which features two structural items or principles which once more show the similarity of traditional printed fiction and the hypertextual text we are discussing.

Firstly, the reader is presented with an introduction which sets the tone for the further development of the work. Underneath a short quotation from Thomas PYNCHON, which is actually the famous passage on ignorance from his *Slow Learner*[1] edition, the authors have arranged a rather paratactic text about knowing, remembering, and thinking. At the bottom of the page the reader finds the main navigation which lets him enter this hypertext.

The categories are red ("sickening decadent hypertext novel"), purple ("metafictional bullshit"), blue ("sort of a documentary"), orange ("correspondence"), brown ("art is cool look at art"), and green ("live readings"). By providing these, the authors offer the reader six points which branch off into more diversified subtrees. Yet again, this 'table-of-contents'-approach clearly refers back to printed tradition, enabling readers to track the desired pieces of information more quickly and easily.

This method clearly refers to what STORRER has termed 'structure overviews', al-

---

[1] http://www.pynchon.pomona.edu/slowlearner/rose.html, accessed 25.04.05

Figure 6.2.

"*The Unknown*- Main navigation"

lowing the reader to get information as to the overall size of the work and to position himself in the network of lexias.

The first category entitled "The Red Line: Parts of Their Story"[2] comprises about 300 entries, which can be clicked in order to access the individual fragments. These, in turn, contain written text covering from one half to a whole monitor-frame. Quite a number of words and phrases are marked as links. Interestingly, already from looking at this overall structure and the individual design of the fragments, we can identify three different methods of navigating through the network and read the text.

The most obvious method is to refer to the main table-of-contents (TOC), click on a heading, read the fragment that opens up and, after reading, use the browser's back-button in order to come back to the TOC and enter another fragment. Using this method, one can read all textual items without even the slightest danger of 'getting lost'. Here, it is possible for the reader to work his way from top to bottom, and with little effort he can skip headings which do not sound so interesting, or read them in reverse order. As far as the authors' intention of structuring or ordering the 300 headings is concerned, an instructive discovery can be made when looking at the source code of the TOC-page: The file-names are ordered alphabetically, in other words, there does not seem to be an organising principle at work that is connected to the content of the individual fragments. Unless the authors have not made an effort to think about a proper order, and then attributed the respective file-names in order to maintain this order, I

---

[2]`http://www.unknownhypertext.com/redline.htm`, accessed 25.04.05

suggest that we can suitably attribute the label 'random' to the order presented. This thesis can also be supported when looking at the way in which *The Unknown* is being created: Since the work seems to be in a flux and new pieces are added continuously, it would be quite uneconomic for the writers to rename all the files each time there is the need to fit in a specific new item between two existing ones.

The authors themselves are quite outspoken about the production process of their hypertext. Following a link on the "orange-line" ("correspondence"), William GILLESPIE writes:

> I've been working hard on the Unknown for a few days. I didn't mean to. It just happened. Here's a list of new scenes I uploaded just now:
>
> angels.htm
>
> blame.htm
>
> conspiracy.htm
>
> (kind of a basement tape, this one has no links in except the Red Line, and no links out save the navbar)
>
> dac1999a.htm, etc.
>
> discgolf1.htm, etc.
>
> (I have some images for this one I will upload soon)[...][3]

There are, however, some minor exceptions to the phenomenon of randomness just presented, which also leads our discussion towards the second method of browsing *The Unknown*. Again referring to the source-code of the TOC-file, we recognise that some file-names carry an internal order, they are named `halloween2.htm`, `halloween3.htm`, `halloween4.htm` for example. Correspondingly, the respective headings are "Halloween - We Stole a Good Idea From Mary Shelley", "Halloween - It Was a Dark and Stormy Night", "Halloween - The NSCA is like Star Trek", and so forth. When accessing these fragments, the navigational links "NEXT" respectively "PREVIOUS" appear at the bottom of the screen, implying a kind of linear interrelationship between these fragments. Hence, by means of these links one can move back and forth through a chain of

---

[3]`http://www.unknownhypertext.com/finishing.htm`, accessed 25.04.05

about five lexias. As far as the content is concerned, however, these modules are only remotely connected. Although they all contain a plot that is connected to Halloween in the broadest sense, they are not part of a larger narrative entity which seems to have been cut into pieces on first sight.

Thirdly, the most random navigational method uses the links within the individual fragments. Here, the underlined words and the modules which are accessed when clicking them refer to each other content-wise in a very obvious way - I stress this feature because this is not always the case in hypertexts, as we will see with regard to some other texts. The first two sentences of "Tomorrow We Start the Tour"[4] for instance contains three links:

> Tomorrow <u>we start our tour</u>. I sure am excited. I doubt Ill get much sleep. I have to try not to drink too much on this <u>tour</u>, or <u>do much in the way of drugs</u>.

Respectively, the three links open a fragment that describes the first stop of the book-tour in Illinois, one that summarises what this tour is all about and how the hypertext is written 'on the go', and the last one describing an accident in connection with the usage of LSD. In other words, as far as linking is concerned, the plot is forwarded by key-words or key-phrases which are used 'pars-pro-toto' (as a synecdoche) in order to further go into specific parts of the text. Hence, the links can be clicked intuitively, and the reader's expectations about what the target he chooses will be are predictable.

Hypertextual characteristics *The Unknown* also makes a valid case for the effective use of multimedial items. As has been mentioned before, the 'leitmotif' of the work is the book-tour through the United States. In the cities the authors visit, they give live-readings of their hypertext. Reading the online-version of the text, the reader gets the chance to actually become a listener: When clicking the "Audio"-button on the right-hand side of the frame, which is accompanied by the exact date and place the recording has been produced, it is possible to hear one of the authors reading out the

---

[4]`http://www.unknownhypertext.com/tomorrow.htm`, accessed 25.04.05

text of the particular module one has just accessed. The transformation of a written text to a performed one is creatively done by hitting a little bell each time a link is reached. During the various performances, the audience is invited to chose which link to visit next when this bell rings.

Another very obvious form of cross-mediality in *The Unknown* are the items which can be accessed via "The Brown Line". Here, the authors have chosen various artworks in order to complement their hypertext. For example, "Katie Gilligans Watercolor Diaries" leads the reader to a fragment enabling him to access about 120 water-colour paintings, each arranged as to symbolise one day between April 28th and August 29th, 1997. Regarding the artist, there is no reference made as to why her images have been integrated into the hypertext. Also, there does not seem to be an inherent connection between the painted images and the rest of the hypertext. I suggest that this adds to the overall characteristics of a "collage" kind of work, and we can imagine how the authors have got to know the painter on the tour and in the process added her pictures to their text. Besides, by including these images, the authors add an intertextual layer to their work by connecting it to 'graphic' text outside of the plot. A similar strategy is the use of citations from other literary works, such as the one by PYNCHON at the very beginning of the work. Referring back to the discussion of the subject in Chapter 3.5, using JAKOB's term we could argue that the latter is a good example of 'deictic intertextuality', contributing to contextualising *The Unknown*. Other multi-media items are connected to the motif of *The Unknown* in a more obvious way. The link "The Blue Cards" takes the reader to the scanned images of note cards with little stories written on them, which are the results of a game the authors describe like this:

> This is game that Dirk, Scott, William, and Anne Bargar made up and played in December of 1997. We took a stack of blue notecards, each took five of them, wrote titles, and then shuffled them in a deck, dealt them out, and wrote little stories for about two hours. The only rules were that you had to write something

from the title, and you could not get your own title.[5]

What is especially interesting about this concept is the fact that here we are presented with what could almost be called 'analogue hypertext', something we referred to in the Chapter 2.3 on 'konzeptionelle Hypertextualität' before. Individual, self-contained textual fragments are created by the authors and written down on a paper-medium. The only thing lacking here to make it a real hypertext would be to interconnect these cards by pieces of thread or establish the links in text-form. These notecards increase the self-reflexivity and metafictional character of the whole work.

Following the high degree of interlinking and the various methods by means of which one can browse the work, we can state that user-participation is highly encouraged. There are only some minor instances where the reader has the chance to let the text proceed on its own, when for example he clicks on a link and listens to a live sound-recording of the authors. However, *The Unknown* generally speaking can be characterised by its high degree of interactivity. Furthermore, the arrangement of the fragments the work consists of clearly forwards its non-linearity or *Mehrfachsequenziertheit*. On the inter-fragmental level, the reading can be performed in random order, thus leaving it up to the reader how he would like to approach the text.

In Chapter 3.6 we have examined the relationship between open and closed structures within hypertexts. Despite the fact that the authors are adding fragments to their work continually, the borders of the text itself remain identifiable because intertextual items occur relatively sparsely. Almost all fragments are connected to the motif of the book-tour and written by the authors themselves. As a consequence, establishing the textual delineations of *The Unknown* is largely unproblematic.

As regards the discussion of the hypertextual characteristics and their function in the present work, the last question which needs to be scrutinised is which effect these have

---

[5]`http://www.unknownhypertext.com/games.htm`, accessed 25.04.05

6. Analysis

for the reception of the text. I suggest that because of the omnipresence of the main-navigation and the often "predictable" way of linking the individual anecdotes together, the authors support the creation of coherent readings of the narrative. This view is also held by JENSEN [50] in his thesis *Internet Hyperfiction. Can it ever Become a Widely Popular Artform?*:

> This hyperfiction worked better for me than the ones that try so hard to subvert the conventions of print literature. For me it is the hyperfictions that work best in practise, both in terms of entertainment and experimentation with the medium, which should be developed further.

The author also bases this conclusion on the analysis of the narrative properties of the text, which we will turn to in the next paragraph.

Narrative On the story level, I would first of all like to refer to the 'events' which characterise *The Unknown*. As has been outlined before in Chapter 5, since the work belongs to the genre of the travelogue, there are quite a number of events which are all contained within the individual lexias that construct this piece of hyperfiction. These modules are so numerous that it would be far beyond the scope of this thesis to refer to them all - even more so because all of them represent independent entities that can be analysed one by one. On the intrafragmental level, events are contained within individual fragments, making them appear like self-contained very short stories. This independence is also reflected on the interfragmentary level: referring to the causality of the events, we can state that we cannot find connections between the individual elements whatsoever. The only indication of an implicit order within the text is conveyed by the use of dates and times. By writing different 'scenes' - as the authors also refer to them - in a diary-like manner, the reader is enabled to reconstruct the temporal relationship of the events he encounters when browsing the hypertext.

As far as the settings are concerned, they are usually locations visited by the authors during their book-tour, such as Cincinnati, Buffalo, and Chicago. These 'real' places parallel the cast of 'real' characters occurring in the autobiographical anecdotes: Apart from the four authors, hypertext theorists and writers such as Shelley JACKSON, Komninos ZERVOS, and Thomas PYNCHON and Don DELILLO appear.

In order to shed some light on the discourse level of *The Unknown*, I should like to start with discussing the aspect of 'order'. From the discussion of the navigational strategies the text supports, it has already become evident that it can be browsed in random order because its individual textual fragments are independent entities which invite non-linear reading. On the intrafragmental level, however, the text is organised in a linear fashion and bears no difference to traditional printed literature. The relationship between the textual fragments also has consequences for the work's duration. While the duration of the authors' reading tour spans a number of years, the discourse represents an acceleration, omitting the events which occur outside the book-tour and thus the 'space' of the narrative. Here, it is possible to identify the duration of the whole work as summary and ellipsis.

The class of 'frequency' is wholly dependent on how the textual network is being traversed. Since we are dealing with a rhizomatic structure here, it is possible to encounter the same fragment more than once. As a result, the same event is told several times, i.e. the discourse is repetitive.

The characters of the work are mostly presented in a showing mode, each fragment and each anecdote revealing different traits of the characters. This is, however, only true with regard to the protagonists of the story - the other characters (real people) are mostly referred to quite rarely, thus rendering them 'flat'. In my opinion, good examples for the showing mode are the fragments in which the protagonists engage in discussions:

> William has a tattoo, too, I note, of Gertrude Steins head, freshly cut into the flesh over his left shoulder blade.
>
> "Thats new," says I.
>
> "I got drunk in Tiajuana [sic]," says William, " "with some lesbian bikers. You like?"

I nod my head, though Im not crazy about the tattoo. Stein's cool and all, but her head on your shoulder? It says, "Yes we have no bananas today," underneath the head. Which wasn't an original Stein line, anyway. But I wasn't going to bring that up. Not now.

"You wanna jump?" asks William.[6]

In contrast, there are also a few instances where the prevailing mode of characterisation is that of telling:

Mike was eager to be our chauffeur through Colorado. He had written some of my lines, I had rewritten some of his sentences, and he was a great researcher and avid reader of the news. Which is not even to mention a swell guy, a pal's pal.[7]

As can be already guessed from the initial motivation for the creation of *The Unknown* as a joint effort by four authors, the mode of the discourse is multi-perspectival and homodiegetic. The authors develop the story of their reading tour by contributing individual perspectives to the narrative.

Regarding focalisation, the text on the initial screen, for example, is written from the point of view of a detached focaliser who reflects on the concept of things "unknown". This metafictional element in a self-reflective way comments on the discourse, and the narrator can here be described as being heterodiegetic. At one stage, in a fragment called "Collective Conclusion or Prologue", the authors reflect on the aspects of the literary process they are involved in:

What is clear is that if hypertext hopes to become something more than an essentially obscure academic subspecialty, it will need to have some readers, ideally the kind of readers without advanced degrees. The kind of people who read books on trains and beaches. The kind of people who read for fun, not for a living. That's how you build a literature.

---

[6]http://www.unknownhypertext.com/bungie2.htm, accessed 25.04.05
[7]http://www.unknownhypertext.com/colorado.htm, accessed 15.06.05

6. Analysis

The perspective changes when the reader enters one of the navigational strands that have been outlined before. Here, the narrator is homodiegetic.

> One of my checking accounts is dead and bleeding a trickle of pennies. The other is new, it has $75. To last for food for ten days. I just got the cash card in the mail yesterday. But when I opened it today I discovered that the Personal Identification Number (PIN) was following in a separate mailing. Which I did not receive in today's mail. It is after noon on Saturday and all the branches of the credit union are closed so I cannot make a withdrawal. Perhaps there is someplace I can cash a check but I don't know where, and already the thought that I am having to resort to means of squeezing money out of my accounts that I have never resorted to before, all to drive in a car with squishy, scraping brakes to the third-largest city in America to go to a party, albeit a very cool one, is making me uncomfortable.[8]

The mode of discourse, as can be already guessed from the preceding discussion, is quite heterogeneous, in that the work is presented using different communicative techniques. For instance, we can find modules containing direct speech, a purely descriptive mode as well as letter- and email-communication and even song-lyrics.[9] I believe it therefore to be justified to refer to this phenomenon as a 'multi-modal' presentation. Once more, this element of the discourse reflects the overall collage-like structure of the narrative.

Finally, I would like to highlight the style that is used by the authors, which is called "[...] youthful and vibrant [...]" by JENSEN [50]. Parallel to the different modes that can be identified in the discourse, there is also a lot of variation regarding the language that is being used. For example, in a fragment called "Dirk's Will", the author uses quite a legal and conventionalised style:

> I, "Dirk," being of sound mind (the body being in dispute, given my status as a

---

[8]http://www.unknownhypertext.com/regret.htm, accessed 30.04.05

[9]cf. http://www.unknownhypertext.com/gospel4.htm, accessed 25.04.05

fiction) in anticipation of that event that comes to us all, now set forth my last will and testament. If I die there will be little doubt that the responsible parties will include my partners William Gillespie and Scott Rettberg. Despite this, I hereby appoint them as executors of my estate [...][10]

Quite differently, in another fragment slang and swear-words are being used:

"Fuckers," Louis said, bringing from his disc bag a shining serrated buzzsaw blade, and sighting along it toward the men below.

"Are they following us?" I asked. "Should we offer to let them play through?"

"Fuck it," Louis said. "Let's just get going."[11]

Thus, next to being multi-modal, the present discourse can also be said to be multi-stylistic.

Aarseth's typology Since we are presented with a highly complex structure in this work, with multiple entrance and exit-points, the internal organisation of *The Unknown* is indeterminable. Another characteristic is that, unless the user clicks on a link explicitly, the work will not be forwarded. Therefore, the text is intransient. A slight exception, as could be argued, are the little insertions of audio-fragments; indeed, when activating one of these sound-files, the user has to wait until the file has been played, this cannot be influenced. Regarding text access, we can give the label 'random'. As shown before, the reader sees a table of contents on the initial page, leading him to a more detailed overview of the individual fragments, which he can all choose from at will. Finally, in this work, there are only explicit links, leading users to the same pages every time.

Suter's typology Therefore, as far as the overall structure of the work is concerned, using SUTER's categories, this work could be referred to as a rhizome. Once the user has entered a specific textual fragment, he is able to continue his reading in an almost endless

---

[10]http://www.unknownhypertext.com/dirkwill.htm, accessed 25.04.05

[11]http://www.unknownhypertext.com/discgolf4.htm, accessed 25.04.05

fashion by activating the links that the authors have added to their text. However, as we have seen in the discussion above, because of the various ways in which *The Unknown* can be navigated through, it would be possible to suggest that traces of a tree-structure are also present since one can use the TOC-pages to enter the main categories of the work.

6.3. These Waves of Girls

⇒ Author: Caitlin FISHER

⇒ Award: 2001 ELECTRONIC LITERATURE AWARD for fiction

⇒ ELO category: Hypertext fiction, Recorded Readings/Performances of Fiction

General description and technology   Tracey, the narrator in this work of hyperfiction, describes how she has come to terms with her homosexuality and explores her childhood for markers of this development. The work can be described as being a collection of anecdotes and memories. It relies on standard HTML-programming, including frames, images, and a number of soundfiles that are either background noises accompanying the respective scenes or live readings of the text, presumably by the author herself. Quite similar to *The Unknown*, all the scenes are interlinked but can also be read following the main categories given in the main navigation.

The events are mostly memories from Tracey's childhood. Moreover, the scenes she presents mostly deal with the (sexual) relationships between the girls and boys of her age. This can be fittingly demonstrated when referring to the following sample. Here, the author describes an event which happened when she was ten years old. A couple of girls chase a boy on their bikes, finally catch him, take his clothes of him and leave him in a sandpit where they kick sand into his face.

> As the sand clears, he's crumbling and sobbing and we seem so much bigger than he is, there, like a shell-less thing, his penis coated with gravel. And he wasn't supposed to be that small. [12]

Here, one clearly sees the power-relationship between boys and girls of Tracey's childhood, being completely opposite to the notion of men belonging to the "strong" sex. As far as the character of the boy is concerned, he remains nameless and does not reappear in any of the other fragments, which is typical of the set-up of the present work.

---

[12]`http://www.yorku.ca/caitlin/waves/vanessa.htm`, accessed 26.04.05

Navigation and linking   The work is introduced by a splash screen showing a little animation with the camera flying through a cloudy sky. In the background, we hear a looped sound of laughing girls, so the overall tone that is set from the beginning is a rather joyful and optimistic one. Bibliographical data as well as the fact that this work has won the *2001 ELECTRONIC LITERATURE AWARD for fiction* are also included.

After a couple of seconds, the reader is automatically forwarded to the second screen, which could roughly be described as a table of contents (Figure 6.3) by means of which the reader can access various parts of this narrative. Interestingly, it is not possible to skip the initial screen, the reader has to wait until the introductory splash screen changes.

When moving the mouse over the button titled "Listen", a tree-structure appears, containing links to the various main parts of the story as well as short introductory abstract that also pops up when selecting an item of this structure. This lexia could be referred to as the main table-of-contents and serves as a structure overview in order for the reader to be able to estimate the extent of *These Waves of Girls*. Furthermore, the author has also included local context cues in her work: When the reader moves the mouse across an item of this structure overview, a text box pops up, containing the first lines of the fragment which will open when this respective link is being clicked, providing the reader with an information as to what he has to expect from choosing the one or the other link.

As regards the word "listen" which opens up the table-of-contents, right from the beginning, the author suggests that the mode of transmission of this story is going to be aural - at least partly. And indeed, at various stages the reader is able to access soundfiles containing readings of the lexias.

On moving into the text by choosing "kissing girls", the reader accesses a page containing a navigational menu on the left hand side, and the blurred image of two girls kissing in the main frame. On clicking the first item, "Vanessa", the hypertext offers a written text interspersed with a number of images, beside others containing the link

"Would you rather listen to the story?". On mouse-over a sound-file can be heard, with the author reading out the first couple of lines from the text. Here, the author reverses the usual conventions of browsing the internet: usually, the mouse-over[13] does not in itself trigger an event, in other words, the sudden start of the sound comes at a surprise. When the user actually clicks this link, he can then choose between various sound files being read out loud to him.

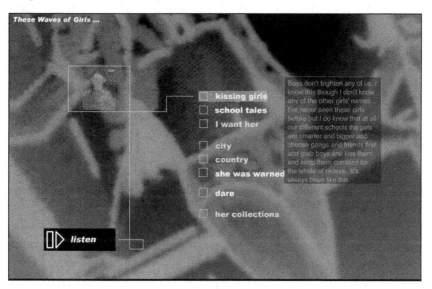

Figure 6.3.

"These Waves of Girls - Table of Contents"

In order to have a closer look at the function of links in the present text, I would like to refer to a closer analysis performed by SIMANOWSKI [80], which is one of the very few closer readings of hypertextual fiction on the internet found in secondary literature:

In einem Node erfahren wir Traceys Wunschtraum, ins Bett der heimlich geliebten

---

[13]The pointer of the mouse is moved over the respective part of the page , e.g. a link or an image. No button is being clicked. For a link - if the programmer has used this function - a little yellow box pops up containing the name of the link. Also, in the bottom-left bar of the browser screen, we can see the actual path the link will take us to.

Lehrerin zu kriechen[14]. Der Node linkt zu Traceys Großmutter, mit der sie sich als Kind im Bett Geschichten erzählte, und dieser Node beginnt bezeichnenderweise mit den Worten: "I am growing up but not out of my grandmother's bed." Der Link verbindet zunächst einfach zwei Bettszenen. Im vorliegenden Falle kann oder muss man ihn allerdings auch als eine Erklärung lesen, als eine Erklärung der erotischen Phantasie von heute aus den Kuschelstunden von damals. Der Link wandelt sich von der Kunjunktion und zur Konjunktion weil: Es gibt den erotischen Tagtraum, ins Bett der Lehrerin zu kriechen, weil die Erfahrung der Stunden im Bett der Großmutter das Gefühlsleben der Jungen Tracy unauslöschlich geprägt haben. [...]

A good example of how links are used in an ironic way in this piece of hyperfiction is how Tracey associates the darkness of a cinema with a forest at night. In hand_travels2.htm, where she describes an episode when a man sitting next to her in a cinema tries to touch her knees, the phrase the theatre was so dark is linked to a fragment containing the image of a forest and the written text "At night the fireflies come out. They make me squirm, so beautiful at night [...]"[15]. Hence, the disturbing and uncomfortable feeling of getting touched by a stranger in a dark cinema is ironically juxtaposed to a sense of beauty and tranquility conveyed by the fireflies in nature.

Hypertextual characteristics The author appears to use many techniques - especially those involving different types of media - in order to achieve the desired artistic effects. It is also because of this mixture of media that the work acquires a sense of collage and fragmentation. Here, it is especially remarkable to note that the author uses graphical images functioning as links which, when being clicked, lead to a target-fragment that once again consists of a graphical image exclusively. In other words, rather than merely supporting what is being expressed in the written text, the graphics prominently carry information that forward the plot. This is visible for instance in a number of fragments starting with birchstand1.htm, where the author describes a forest and the reader needs

---

[14]http://www.yorku.ca/caitlin/waves/tell10.htm
[15]http://www.yorku.ca/caitlin/waves/farm_fireflies.html, accessed 25.04.05

to click through a series of pictures of a forest before he can continue reading written text.

The work requires a high degree of user-interaction, apart from the few examples where an audio-file is being played and the reader has to wait until it is finished. In contrast to *The Unknown*, however, the present work features many longer fragments which need to be scrolled down on the screen. Thus, structurally speaking, since the author employs several longer successional fragments, the reading mode becomes less interactive: although links are being offered to lead the reader to other lexias, he or she is also encouraged to read the fragment until the end. Curiously, on some occasions the author has arranged portions of text underneath each other, although in this case hypertext-convention would have it that these are all cut apart, distributed in the textual space and interconnected by links. In `tammy_stevens.htm`, for instance, this is not the case. Rather, the author opts for arranging the fragments underneath each other, achieving a sense of linearity. Hence, although the work is a rhizome (and thus *per definitionem* multi-sequential/non-linear) and can be browsed in random order, the author uses strategies in order to evoke a sense of linearity. This is achieved mainly by the use of 'previous' and 'next'-buttons, an example of which will be analysed in the next paragraph.

Regarding the characteristic of intertextuality, I suggest that in the present work the author does not integrate references to other, surrounding texts. This fact reinforces the notion that *These Waves of Girls* creates a textual world of its own, making no use of links to websites or other sources. As a consequence, the work is a very closed text and it is easy to trace its delineations, i.e. what still belongs to this text and what needs to be attributed to one "next to it". For this reason, it would be possible to publish this work on a data medium other than the internet: Similar to CD-ROM hyperfiction, it could also run on a local computer. Hence I suggest that the production process of the present text can be compared to that of a printed publication. The splash screen found at the very beginning provides information as to the title of the work, its author, the date of publication, the fact that the work has been awarded the ELO-award for fiction, the writer's email-address and - quite tellingly - a genre-affiliation: Fisher calls her work *A Hypermedia Novella*. Hence, the work quite consciously employs conventions of traditional printed literature in order to emphasise its referentiability and fixity.

This technique - as well as the hypertextual characteristics mentioned above - influences the way in which *These Waves of Girls* is received by the audience. For one, because of longer narrative fragments and the clear navigational structure, the reader can construct a coherent reading without a lot of cognitive effort. In addition, it is possible for him to identify the work "as such", i.e. he is made aware of the text-borders, which again facilitates the reading of the work.

Narrative The narrative, for these reasons, can be analysed parallel to *The Unknown* because it also consists of individual independent episodes represented in the fragments. Characters appearing in these fragments are not further developed on an interfragmental basis, rather, they appear only within single fragments and as a result, remain flat characters.

Regarding the story level, I would first of all like to have a closer look at the events and the existents in *These Waves of Girls*.

In a series of fragments starting with `beamroutine1.htm`, Tracey describes a part of the story which spans a number of successive fragments:

> Fifteen. I am at that Chateau St. Louis jazz bar drinking strawberry daiquiries with Vivian.
>
> We have nothing in the fridge at home, nothing ... just candied sprinkles, one pop tart, two packages of chicken-noodle cup-a-soup.[16]

At the bottom of the page, the reader can see a small icon of an arrow pointing to the right, indicating that by clicking it he will be forwarded to the next fragment containing a continuation of the introduction he has read. As we have seen in the discussion of *The Unknown*, the authors also employed this sort of navigational 'previous' and

---

[16]`http://www.yorku.ca/caitlin/waves/beamroutine1.htm`, accessed 25.04.05

'next'-buttons. However, whereas in the latter narrative the ensuing fragment was not connected to the previous content-wise, the reader finds a development of the plot in *These Waves of Girls*. Tracey and her friend Vivian visit the described bar, where the former admits her having fallen in love with the latter. In the course of the plot, Tracey gets involved with a shoe-salesman who has paid for a couple of her drinks. However, rather than having sex with him ("I don't want to have sex," I say. "Not with you."[17]), she performs her beam-routine naked while he masturbates.

> I take off my clothes and, fifteen, mount the line of the carpet, perform my entire junior beam routine, handstand press, two backhandsprings included.He jerks off. Dismount.

> I hurry into my clothes and head home to Vivian (who loves me, but not as much as I love her). For years I worry that the shoe salesman was really really disappointed, stuck with a fifteen year old virgin gymnast rather than a real bad girl.[18]

Here, the series of events spans eight fragments and form a plot in itself in that they are temporally and causally connected to each other in a meaningful way. Although these fragments contain a number of links encouraging the reader to diverge, at the same time the very arrangement of the fragments suggest a linear reading of the plot.

As far as the characters of the story are concerned, they are only important in so far as they contribute to the characterisation of Tracey the narrator. Consequently, these characters remain flat and are not developed in the course of the narration. What needs to be emphasised here is the way in which girls seem to dominate the world of the author's childhood:

> Boys don't frighten any of us. I know this though I don't know any of the other girls' names... I've never seen these girls before but I do know that at all our different schools the girls are smarter and bigger and choose gangs and friends

---

[17]http://www.yorku.ca/caitlin/waves/beamroutine8.htm),accessed25.04.05
[18]Ibid.

first and grab boys and kiss them and keep them corralled for the whole of recess.

It's always been like this.

Accordingly, the female characters - from a narrative point of view - seem to be slightly more developed and 'round', one reason being that most of them are the focus of Tracey's affection. Male characters are almost treated with a dismissive tone of voice, which will become clear in the next paragraph discussing the way in which the characters are presented on the discourse level. In order to conclude the analysis of the story-level, I would like to refer to the settings of the work. Here, we can roughly pinpoint rural Canada because at one stage Tracey and Vivian are referred to as "the little Quebecois girls"[19].

From the main navigational menu the reader can access the links "city" and "country". When selecting the former, the reader enters a series of lexias which, beside others, also contain the beam-routine strand discussed earlier on. The latter transports the reader to a series of fragments which are all connected to nature and the countryside.

> We had a farm with swings and a feather bed, tall trees like France, apple trees
>
> lining the roadway. We had a metal gate and two barns - one filled with old cars
>
> - and one with a kid's tricycle from the turn of the century.[20]

However, these two links are comparably "eventless" in comparison to other strands such as "kissing girls" and "school-tales". Here, the most important setting is school. Tracey describes her teachers and her class-mates, drawing special attention to the girls and the female teachers. It is made clear that this environment represents the center of the narrator's memories and that the motif of teaching and learning - in the sense of coming to terms with one's sexuality - is of crucial importance for the reading of her work.

Referring to the level of discourse permits us to first refer to the order of events. As has been suggested before, the work can be read in random order because of its navigational structure. Nonetheless, the reader is provided with some information enabling him to

---

[19]http://www.yorku.ca/caitlin/waves/banana_apples.htm, accessed 25.04.05

[20]http://www.yorku.ca/caitlin/waves/farm.htm, accessed 25.04.05

locate the respective fragment on the temporal axis. In most of the scenes in school for example, the reader is informed about which grade Tracey and her friends were in when the respective event occurred. Also, in the beam-routine scene mentioned above, we get to know that she is fifteen years old at that stage. In this scene, moreover, we find an instance of retroversion:

> Vivian is really really good at this. She spreads her legs just a little and can
> blush thinking about it. Once some guy saw her on sparks street and bought her
> a guitar. Just like that. He'd sent cheese baskets to the apartment for 2 months.
> Vivian is the kind of girl you'd do that for.[21]

Regarding the frequency of the discourse, it can be noted that - also quite similar to *The Unknown*, the various fragments can be visited more than once, making the discourse repetitive in this context. As for the way in which the characters are described I suggest that because all the persons involved in the scenes Tracey describes are flat characters, they are all directly characterised. Apart from Vivian, the characters only appear once in their respective fragment and as result - because of the lack of narrative space - it is impossible to develop the character in showing mode. In `tammy_stevens.htm` she describes a school-mate:

> Grade five we all knew what a slut was: Tammy Stevens. Tammy was in grade six.
> She'd sit all angelic-like in assembly, cross-legged on the gym floor. She was sitting
> on Ricky Sutherland's hand. I'm serious. We were grossed out and fascinated. I
> went home and practiced sitting on my hand. It didn't seem worth it, somehow.
> Ricky Sutherland went around talking like having a girl sit on his hand meant he
> wasn't a virgin anymore.

And a little bit further on in the same fragment it says:

> Tammy Stevens went all the way. In February. In the snow. Ricky Sutherland
> and Tammy broke up – she was way too slutty even for him.

---

[21]`http://www.yorku.ca/caitlin/waves/beamroutine3.htm`, accessed 25.04.05

In this fragment, two characters appear who are not referred to anywhere else in this piece of hyperfiction. Tammy is merely characterised by her being a "slut", and her boyfriend Ricky in turn is only characterised via her. In other words, the reader's impression of the two remains extremely superficial, their only function being the forwarding of the plot.

The discourse is narrated by Tracey who is both the homodiegetic narrator as well as the internal focaliser. Using the past-tense exclusively, she recounts the events that have happened to and around her from her own point of view. Also, the text features some metafictional elements, where the point of view is shifted and the narrator reflects on the act of writing:

> I write, but it doesn't need to be my life, exactly. It lets me fill in the parts I forget. One name. One moment . A hand on my thigh that reminds me of all the other hands. Of yours.[22]

Finally, the mode of narration is a descriptive account of events which have happened in the past in the mode of a summary, including only the episodes of the narrator's memory that are evidently important to her. Regarding the style of the narrative, it is written in simple prose, resembling the way in which one would write a diary.

Aarseth's typology As far as the determinability of the present text is concerned, I suggest that the traversal function is determinable. Although a click on a link might lead to a totally different part of the network, the cause-and-effect sequence always stays the same. Furthermore, as in *The Unknown*, the text is intransient, apart from the few occasions where a sound-file is being played and the user cannot influence the succession of an event or of events. This characteristic is especially visible at the very beginning of the work, where the reader has to listen to the laughter of the girls and to watch the clouds passing by, before being forwarded to the story automatically.

Arguably, access in this text is controlled. Although the user can choose between the main categories, he then finds himself in a rather labyrinthine structure, so it is no

---

[22]http://www.yorku.ca/caitlin/waves/hand_on_my_thigh.htm, accessed 25.04.05

longer possible to individually choose one specific textual fragment. Linking is explicit, the links will always transport the reader to the same part of the narrative and are not influenced by the navigational strategy the user has followed.

Suter's typology The present work is clearly a rhizome: After having started one's reading of the text, there is virtually an infinite number of possible paths to take. The browsing through the structure is helped by a navigational menu on the left-hand side of the screen which is always visible. The contents of the fragments often allude to the menu items (or vice versa), so that in effect the reader is provided with enough information in order not to get lost in the hypertext. Hence, it also justified to say that we can find traces of a tree structure here as well: Starting from the eight main categories of the second index-page one can enter various textual strands. However, in contrast to a real tree-structure, these strands are all interconnected and make *These Waves of Girls* a rhizome.

The reader very quickly makes the observation that the motif of *These Waves of Girls* is the narrator's memory of her childhood. For a number of reasons, then, the topic of memory is also very well suited for being worked into a piece of hypertext. Firstly, a person's memory is, by definition, formed out of individual fragments, anecdotes, and episodes. Hence, the way the human brain organises - or rather stores - the information received largely resembles what Caitlin FISHER has tried to do in her work. She presents pieces of her own memory and her individual perception of the events she encountered, and leaves it to the reader to form his own sequential reading of the events.

Also, I suggest that hypertext is ideally suited for presenting one's memory because the information stored is not only received and interpreted language, but also sounds and images. The author, therefore, employs a wide range of multi-medial items in order to make her work resemble the narrator's memory as closely as possible. So for instance, the sound of laughing girls the reader can listen to at the beginning of the text is, arguably, quite likely to stem directly from the narrator's recollection. In this manner, we can go even a step further and suggest that some of images FISHER uses are blurred because the memory, in this respect, is also not so clear: Images - and memories - melt into each other.

6.4. My Boyfriend came back from the War

⇒ Author: Olia LIALINA

⇒ ELO category: Hypertext fiction

General description and technology *My Boyfriend came back from the War* is by now a classic piece of hyperfiction, written by Russian author Olia LIALINA in 1996. In her text, the narrator describes the first moments between a couple after the boy has just returned from the war, in a series of short textual fragments. In the course of the plot, the girl admits that she has had an affair with her neighbour.

The author makes heavy use of frames in her work, and thus subdivides the screen into many portions, which is the main structural feature of this narrative, which is shown in Fig. 6.4. After having entered the text, the reader can follow the plot within one of the parts of the screen, until he reaches the end. Some of his decisions alter the content of another frame, so that the whole structure is reminiscent of a labyrinth. The user follows the path of the plot across the structure, finally reaching the end-screen, which he encounters at any rate. Moreover, there is no way of getting back in the structure as the work is organised in such a way that the user clicks his way from the entry point to the end of each strand of action. This end is also very clearly marked since once the reader has clicked through the sequence of fragments, the result is only a black background.

Navigation and linking In comparison to the works we have analysed before with regard to the navigational tools they make use of, *My Boyfriend came back from the War* features neither a menu nor a table-of-contents to choose from. Quite the contrary, when entering the text, there is only one link to click - the sentence "My boyfriend came back from the war. After dinner they left us alone." After having opened this link, the narrative continues. Here, it is interesting that almost all graphical images and all fragments of written text carry a link. Thus, as far as the interconnection of the individual modules which make up the text is concerned, it has almost reached the maximum possible extent: All the fragments are links leading to fragments which are also links themselves, in other words there is no item that implies stability or the possibility of existing without the surrounding text.

Figure 6.4.

"My boyfriend came back from the war"

Regarding the various possibilities of using links, the author seems to draw the reader into the narrative, and she does this by offering very short sentences and text fragments which are all interlinked to a high degree. The speed of clicking and thus selecting the links is as fast as the reading speed of the average reader itself, thus the work is explored at a very high pace. As a result, we are presented with a very systematic and clear cause-and-effect structure. There are no structure overviews or context-cues included in the narrative, so the reader has to "trust" the author that the results of his interaction with the text leads to results which contribute to coherent readings on his side.

Hypertextual characteristics There are only a few graphical images in the text, and as a result, the most important carrier of information is the white written text on a black background. Thus, the presentation of the text itself, i.e. its layout, is very much iconic in itself, since it reflects the difficult situation the couple finds itself in. Usually, the colour black is associated with death and gloom, which in this example also seems to be the echo of the war that has just been survived by the male character. It follows that the sparse usage of cross-medial items supports the written text and increases the tension of the situation the narrative wants to convey.

The method of linking which the author uses has notable effects on the degree of interaction between the text and the reader. Since virtually every item on screen - both graphical images and written text - carries a link, the reader needs to make decisions continually in order to forward the plot. This is even more underpinned by the fragments' brevity: This piece of hyperfiction features lexias consisting only of a single word, further multiplying the frequency of clicks on the side of the reader.

What is also interesting here is the way in which the author experiments with the concept of linearity: Although the reader can choose between the various frames on screen, these nevertheless follow a certain predetermined path the reader is unable to alter. And because no navigational tools are available to the reader, it is not possible for him to read the fragments in reverse order. This structural principle is that of a labyrinth, which will be highlighted in the last paragraph of this chapter.

As far as the integration of other texts into this hyperfictional work is concerned, there is almost nothing to be found. Concerning the war the boyfriend has returned from, the only reference that is made is the narrator's question "Haven't you seen tigers there?"[23], indicating a remote - even exotic - country the war has been fought in. The lack of intertextual references, then - similar to *These Waves of Girls* - emphasises the work's universal applicability, because the scene that is being described could occur to every couple having gone through similar experiences.

From this it also follows that the present text can be regarded as quite a closed structure. Neither the motif of the narrative nor the overall structure suggest that it is open

---

[23]http://www.teleportacia.org/war/120.htm, accessed 25.04.05

for the addition of new fragments. The text-borders, therefore, are also easy to trace and the work as such is identifiable.

In contrast to the works we have studied so far, this one lacks an introductory screen offering general information about the work which would make it uncomplicated to reference. Rather, the very first sentence of the text is already part of the narrative. Only in a small fragment in the bottom right corner does the author give her name and the date of publication which carry an email-link enabling the readers to get in touch with her. In this respect it is interesting that this latter link is not explicitly marked as bibliographical data, but looks like all the other links in the text. As a result, when clicking through the work, this final link becomes a part of the narrative, and the opening-up of an email-window appears to be a desired ending of the narrative.

The production-technique, especially the way in which the fragments are interlinked influence the reading of *My boyfriend came back from the war*. First of all, the very structure, which is unrhizomatic, reduces the amount of reader decisions and possible discourse-pathways. In effect, the author has more control over how the work is received. Although a navigational menu is missing, the readers are not likely to face incoherent readings because of the quasi-sequential structural layout of the present work.

Narrative In order to embark on a closer inspection of the narrative, I would like to have a close look at the story-level. On the subject of events it can be noted that the most important ones actually precede the narrative: These are the leaving of the boyfriend and the relationship between the girl and her neighbour. The story starts with the boyfriend returning from the war rather unexpectedly, and in the course of the dialogue between the characters (where the reader only gets to know 'her' part and has to imagine 'his' responses) these events are mirrored. Thus, in effect we are introduced to a series of events that are both temporally and causally linked. In this short narrative we can find three characters, one of which - the neighbor - is only mentioned and does not act in the story. The boy and the girl are only shown in the (one-sided) dialogue, the characterisation of both will be referred to later on. Finally, regarding the setting of the story, is not developed at all, as has been noted before. Neither the location of the alleged war nor the place the young soldier returns to are referred to by the narrator. In doing so, the author completely focuses the reader's attention on the dialogue rather than providing geographical information possibly leading to his distraction.

As regards the discourse level, it is first of all necessary to refer to the order of the narrative. Here, because of the internal organisation, the reader cannot influence the series of events so that as a result, these are presented in a predetermined sequence comparable to printed literature. In the discourse we find retroversion in that the relationship between her and her neighbor is addressed, and anticipation regarding the possible wedding of the two (former) lovers. This predetermined order also has implications for the frequency of the narration: As the fragments can only be visited once before they are "clicked away", no repetition occurs.

The two protagonists of the story are exclusively characterised by the way they behave during their talk, i.e. the prevailing mode is that of showing. The girl attempts to calm down her boyfriend and thus save their relationship and even considers wedding ("We'll start a new life"[24]). On the other hand, he is only characterised through her, i.e. by her verbal reactions to what he says. He seems to be reluctant ("May be [sic] you look at me?"[25]) and aggressive ("don't kill"[26]).

Regarding the point of view, it is possible to identify a homodiegetic author taking the position of an internal focaliser. The only time this perspective is shifted to external is with regard to the first sentence, where the scene is introduced. The story is being told from the perspective of the girl. Although the initial setting suggests that, being on their own after dinner, the couple enter a dialogue about what happened while the man was away, the present work only offers what the woman says and asks.

Similarly to *The Unknown*, the present text also offers a perspective which decon-

---

[24]http://www.teleportacia.org/war/144.htm, accessed 25.04.05

[25]http://www.teleportacia.org/war/145.htm, accessed 25.04.05

[26]http://www.teleportacia.org/war/117.htm, accessed 25.04.05

structs the fictional work itself by offering a metafictional perspective. As MEDOSCH
[61] suggests, Olia LIALINA offers some detailed statistics concerning her work, which
enables the reader to take a look behind the scenes.[27] Thus, on a related website the
interested user can access a table listing all the files the work is made of together with
their link-targets, and providing information about the contributors to the text as well
as web-server statistics. We can deduce from this that the author is very aware of the
medium and its internal organisation, and makes this technical information a part of
her fictional work.

The mode as well as the style of the discourse resembles oral communication, featuring
elliptical formulations signifying the dialogue between the two, which is presented in the
mode of a 'scene' because the story-time of the girl speaking and the discourse-time of
the reader reading what she says is almost 1:1. This narrative mode is ideally suited for
a hypertext because it involves interaction from the perspective of the reader. After the
initial situation has been clarified by the author by giving the first sentences, the reader
has to imagine what happens during the conversation of the (former) lovers. Since the
hypertext offers fragments of what the woman says, as a consequence the reader takes
the position of the man automatically. Thus, as the dialogue evolves, it is necessary for
the reader to fill in the gaps by imagining what the man could have said or done in order
to provoke the reaction of the woman that we can read on screen. In other words, there
is a constant oscillating movement between what is on the screen and what is left blank
in order for the dialogue to proceed. The motif of the dialogue and its implied notion
of interactivity, then, is also ideally suited for works of hyperfiction which rely on the
decisions of the readers in order to be shaped.

Aarseth's typology Although the author has made extensive use of frames and the
links connect to fragments which are distributed over the screen, the text is still determinable: The effect of clicking a link remains the same in all circumstances, there is no
randomising integrated. Also, the work is intransient. As has been said before, this is

---

[27]This archive can be accessed via http://myboyfriendcamebackfromth.ewar.ru/archives/.

true in a very strong way, the users' motivation to click is highly encouraged because the discourse is sped up by the occurrence of rather short lexias. Access to the text is controlled: The work provides one point of entry, and one final situation, but the fragments in between cannot be randomly accessed by a site-map or a table of contents. Linking is explicit, regardless of how the reader proceeds the link-targets always remain the same.

Suter's typology I propose that this work is a good example for the 'tentacle'-structure: deriving from a single starting point, the reader makes a decision as to which path he would like to follow at a very early stage. Each of the 'tentacles', moreover, leads to a fixed ending. There are, also, traces of tree structure which I would like to give a small example of. The following item represents a node which branches off into two sub-threads:

> But... it was only once...
> Last summer...
> And if you think...
> Why I should explain?...
> Don't you see?
> [28]

The two threads which develop out of this are:

a) NO NEVER - don't kill - him - them[29]

b) he was my neighbour - forgive - ME

Yet again, when a node is reached that offers a choice of links, one can follow the path one opts for and continue until the end.

---

[28]http://www.teleportacia.org/war/110.htm, accessed 25.04.05
[29]Here, "-" indicate the separations between the individual modules.

6. Analysis

At this point it is surely reasonable to question how the author's decision to fragment her text in such a way determines the reading of her work. I suggest that presenting only fragments of the unfolding dialogue in such a way emphasises the very importance of these fragments. Referring to the example quoted above, for the effect on the reader it makes a difference whether he reads a phrase such as "don't kill" - "him" or "don't kill him". If placed on the screen isolated as it is, "don't kill" almost takes a universal quality and a number of associations are raised: the wish for not killing could be projected on a single person, or the man's past in the war, which was also an experience of death, or even in a more metaphorical sense referring to the end of the relationship. This scope of possibilities is all of a sudden reduced when the word is clicked and the next fragment "him" appears. Similarly, the word "forgive" from the quoted example is used in a more general way before the puzzle is solved.

Isolating individual words or phrases in the graphical layout in order to foreground their importance can of course also be found in traditional printed literature. Especially in poetry, the poet is able to add another level of meaning (and interpretation) to his works by purposefully arranging his lines on the page. With regard to *My Boyfriend came back from the War* we have seen how this principle has been adapted successfully in the new electronic medium.

6.5. kokura

⇒ Authors: Mary-Kim ARNOLD, Matthew DERBY

⇒ Award: trAce/Alt-X Hypertext Competition 1998 Honourable Mention

General description and technology As can be read on the initial page of the piece, the present work is about

> **Kokura:** A Japanese city that was the primary target of the atomic bomb dropped on Nagasaki on August 9, 1945. On that morning, Kokura was shrouded in bad weather, and the mission's commander decided to drop the bomb on the secondary target.

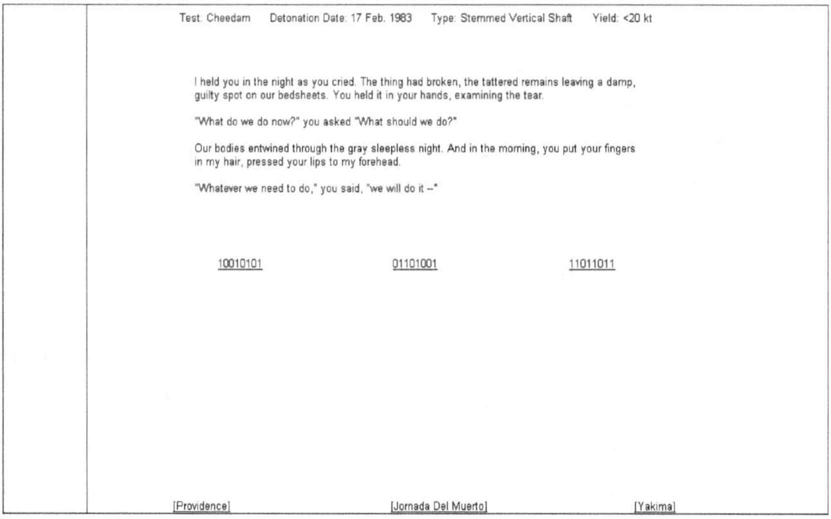

Test: Cheedam   Detonation Date: 17 Feb. 1983   Type: Stemmed Vertical Shaft   Yield: <20 kt

I held you in the night as you cried. The thing had broken, the tattered remains leaving a damp, guilty spot on our bedsheets. You held it in your hands, examining the tear.

"What do we do now?" you asked "What should we do?"

Our bodies entwined through the gray sleepless night. And in the morning, you put your fingers in my hair, pressed your lips to my forehead.

"Whatever we need to do," you said, "we will do it --"

10010101   01101001   11011011

[Providence]   [Jornada Del Muerto]   [Yakima]

Figure 6.5.

"kokura"

The rest of the work, which is told from three different perspectives, however, does not deal with the dropping of nuclear bombs directly, but rather with two characters who meet during anti-war protests. Regarding technology, *kokura* almost entirely relies on short fragments of written text, there are no frames or extensive graphics involved.

Navigation and linking Following this initial statement - which does not contain a link so the reader has to wait for a few seconds before he is forwarded to the next page - is a fragment which could be referred to as the main navigation. On top of the screen the authors have inserted a function which reloads every few seconds and gives the data of various nuclear tests: "Test: Baseball Detonation Date: 05 Feb. 1981 Type: Stemmed Vertical Shaft Yield: 20-150 kt". This information is provided in a loop and hence accompanies every fragment that is accessed subsequently. Underneath the sentence "The beginning of the war will be secret [...]" by American artist Jenny HOLZER, the reader has got the choice between six links, arranged in two lines. On the first line, the cryptic sequences of digits, "10010101", "01101001", and "11011011" mark the entrance points for the three textual strands mentioned above, namely that of the woman, the non-fictional texts, and that of the man. Further down, there are three more links, namely "Providence" which is linked to the initial fragment of the 'woman'-strand, "Jornada Del Muerto" taking the reader to a single lexia containing a black-and-white aerial map of a nuclear testing site in the state of Nevada, and "Yakima" that is connected with the initial module of the man'-strand.

Hypertextual characteristics *Kokura* is a work that lacks graphics almost entirely. The only graphical image the authors offer is the areal black-and-white map of the nuclear testing site in Nevada, the rest being black writing on a white background. In addition to positioning this map in the middle of the screen and making it accessible via a link which is also located centrally, ARNOLD/DERBY make it clear that it also represents the central item of the narrative. This is parallel to what we have found out so far about the characters' relationship and their connection to the anti-war movement.

User-participation in this work can be compared to that of printed literature. Because of the structural setup, which subdivides the narrative into three textual strands, the reader continuously clicks the link at the bottom of each fragment in order to access the ensuing one. Here, the activity of clicking resembles more the leafing through a novel rather than browsing through a hypertext. Thus, within each of the strands, the work presents itself as being sequential, the only exception occurring when the focus is shifted by jumping to and forth between these strands.

Regarding intertextuality, the present work is a good example of how this characteristic of hypertext can be used in order to contextualise a piece of hyperfiction. By integrating newspaper- and TV-reports, the authors firmly set their work in the social and political environment which serves as the background for the love-story of the two protagonists. Furthermore, the constantly-repeated data of the nuclear test-sites at the top of the screen represents a factual background against which the narrative needs to be read. Also, the effect is that non-fictional fragments are integrated into a fictional work, the ease of which is one of the productive advantages of the internet. In the last fragment of the text, therefore, we find a comprehensive list of all the sources which have been used[30], stressing the fact that the authors strive for academic correctness.

As most of the works this presentation discusses, *kokura* also features an initial screen providing its bibliographical data. From this page it can also be gathered that the work is being sponsored by EASTGATE, a publisher focussing on the distribution of CD-ROM hypertexts by Michael JOYCE and Shelley JACKSON. This stability as well as the prevailingly linear mode of the text's traversal lead to easy accessibility of the work by the audience.

Narrative   The first characteristic we need to look at in order to analyse the narrative on the discourse-level is that of order. As we have seen above, the order of events is largely predetermined by the author since the reader is not able to alter the sequence of fragments - and hence events - to a considerable extent. The only choice he is presented with is to start his reading with one of the three strands mentioned above. Having embarked on one of these threads, the reader can also choose to jump back to the very beginning and enter another thread. But in this case, the order of events is not altered, either since the majority of these precede the time the discourse occurs in - the narrative in most parts represents a diary-like account of the past. *Kokura* thus contains a narrative which intermixes events that occur in the present tense, such as the beginning of the daughter's menstruation in the woman's thread ("Momma, I am bleeding," she

---

[30]Cf. http://www.eastgate.com/Kokura/credit.htm, accessed 25.04.05.

whispered. "I am bleeding from down there."[31]) with instances of retrospection ("We stood in long lines, arms linked together."[32]). This order of events also affects the relationship between story- and discourse-time, because the shifting between flashbacks and the "now" functions as a summary of events, therefore leaving gaps and thus accelerating the discourse.

The structural organisation of the hypertext also has effects for the frequency of the discourse. In contrast to *The Unknown* and *These Waves of Girls*, the reader is not confronted with such a high degree of interlinking, and therefore he is less likely to access the same fragment more than once. Repetition in this narrative is not so much dependent on the reader's choices, but rather on the way the authors attempt to describe the same events from different perspectives. Thus, referring to a scene where the activists smear blood on the floor of the Pentagon, this is told from the perspective of the woman, of the man, and of the non-fictional news-report. I will refer to this episode in detail a little bit later on.

Characterisation occurs mainly in an indirect/showing way, by the way the woman and the man describe each other retrospectively. Examples of direct characterisation, however, can also be found in her recollections, when she remembers him describing her outer appearance:

> You once said, "How is it that I am allowed to touch something so perfect, so exquisite, so intricately wrought?" I remember that you said that. Do you remember?[33]

The narrative is being told from three different viewpoints, namely that of a man and woman whose lives are connected by political activism against nuclear proliferation, and a third line that randomly presents excerpts from contemporary media describing the events. These three strands can be read individually - in quite a singular fashion - namely one after another by clicking the respective link that always leads to the successive fragment. Furthermore, the reader also has the possibility to jump between the

---

[31] http://www.eastgate.com/Kokura/woman/woman7.htm, accessed 25.04.05

[32] http://www.eastgate.com/Kokura/woman/woman10.htm, accessed 25.04.05

[33] http://www.eastgate.com/Kokura/woman/woman12.htm, accessed 25.04.05

three strands and thus create a sort of dialogue, especially between the couple.

We are presented with two focalisers who are both part of the story, thus we can talk about a homodiegetic narrative situation here. The author uses a technique which very much fits the communicative characteristics of the internet as the medium. Since the user actively decides which path he would like to follow, i.e. which of the two narrators he would like to listen to, we have in fact a situation of multiple narrators based on the interactive and non-sequential characteristics of hypertext.

The unnamed I-narrator in the woman-plot introduces three other characters: her young daughter (curiously referred to as "Z"), her father who has remarried, and the apparent father of the child she alternately addresses with "you" or "he". Since the fragments of the narrative are arranged in sequence, its construction can be compared to that of a traditional printed text. Hence, successively we get to know that she met her lover during anti-war protests in the United States:

> She found a photo of us, one you had taken, your arm outstretched, back from when we still saw fit to document our time together. We are in front of the reflecting pool. It is summer. I am wearing a blue NOW t-shirt, and my hair is in long braids. You are wearing that brown plaid shirt, and although you can't see it in the picture, I remember that we are holding hands.[34]

In this fragment, the author directly addresses her former lover. There are also cases where this personal relationship is neutralised by means of referring to the lover in third person singular respectively as the father of her child:

> As we had expected, her father has moved to Tokyo. He finally runs his own company now, a division of . . . He writes her letters peppered with Japanese phrases. He is trying to teach her Japanese. He sends her pictures that he has taken of himself – standing in front of McDonald's – "This is the first one built

---

[34]http://eastgate.com/Kokura/woman/woman19.htm, accessed 25.04.05

in Tokyo!" – in the doorway to his office – "See the picture of you I have on my wall!" – with his other children in front of their garden; with his current lover; in front of a fish pond; standing on the subway platform.[35]

Here, we also get to know the fact that the man is of Japanese origin and hence the connection to the overall motif of nuclear bombs dropped on Japanese towns is established.

Correspondingly, the man tells the story from his point of view, including his wife (or current lover, as the woman has referred to her) as well as the woman.

> My wife, Y, is slight and fragile as a paper bird–I love her gently and unerringly to avoid being cut. At night she sings on the porch, if it is warm enough. I watch the back of her head dip and cant, foregrounded by the stars and the city. She is fine enough as a human being, I suppose, but she is nothing I have ever given any thought to in any way, not even as we cake our bodies together in bed [...][36]

Curiously, as we have seen before, the narrator refers to his wife as "Y" similar to the woman who called her daughter "Z" before. Arguably, the narrators would both like to establish a sense of anonymity in a way that the reader's attention is entirely focussed onto the two main characters of *kokura*. This finding is also supported by the encryption of the main-links into the 1 and 0 sequences, as has been referred to before.

Also, the man refers to his former lover:

> I like to think of how you would repond [sic] to this, to my robots, my crisp edges and flaccid excess. You would shudder, I think, at the memory of your hand on my chest, the night we lay on the train tracks, our time in the Nevada desert [...][37]

Furthermore, we can find instances of fragments relating to the same events, being told from both perspectives. Referring to the way in which the peace-protestors sought

---

[35]http://eastgate.com/Kokura/woman/woman17.htm, accessed 25.04.05
[36]http://www.eastgate.com/Kokura/man/man7.htm, accessed 25.04.05
[37]http://www.eastgate.com/Kokura/man/man8.htm, accessed 25.04.05

6. Analysis

to attract the media's (and the government's) attention, both state what follows:

The man:

> We took our own blood and poured it out on the Pentagon floor. We lay out on
> the tracks, across highways, over ground zero [...][38]

The woman:

> In the heat of the summer. My legs, bare. I remember the slickness beneath my
> thighs. The audacity of using our own blood. Sitting, cross-legged on the floor.
> It was impossible not to be heady with it all – the overwhelming smell like warm
> iron, steel. Sticky. Slick. The sense of vitality, of energy in that room, against
> that cold, hard floor, this pool of – we were heady with it all – it was as if you
> could almost hear the pumping of our hearts, see the pulsing – [...][39]

This is only one instance where the narrations of both narrators overlap. If we include the third textual stratum, namely the collection of news-stories about the peace-activists, the internal connections become even more visible. Therefore, although being a hypertext potentially open to a high degree of interlinking, the most important links are established by the contents of fragments and *not* by their "physical" or "technical" interconnection. What is rather untypical of a piece of hyperfiction - the authors leave out the links where they could have been expected by the reader. Links could have been used as metaphors for example, thus closer connecting the three textual strata.

When the man recollects his participation in an action in the Nevada desert, he tells the reader:

> There were shells everywhere, blasted, red remains, half sunk in deep craters. We
> saw houses out there, and cars; test models thrown up to see what would happen.
> We could see the busted remains of them from miles away. Skeletal towers, jeeps,
> the shattered half of a schoolbus.[40]

---

[38]http://www.eastgate.com/Kokura/man/man16.htm, accessed 25.04.05

[39]http://www.eastgate.com/Kokura/woman/woman8.htm, accessed 25.04.05

[40]http://www.eastgate.com/Kokura/man/man14.htm, accessed 25.04.05

The respective news-story reads like this:

> Antinuclear activists extended their protests this week as Congress prepared to consider temporary storage of high-level nuclear waste at the Nevada Test Site. [...]
>
> Less than 100 demonstrators have been arrested so far at the traditional spring antinuclear protests at the NTS gates. They were cited for trespassing and released on Sunday and Friday [...][41]

The mode of the narrative is a mixture between the personal - and rather emotional - recollections of the two former lovers and the news-reports underpinning the social and political relevance of the actions they had participated in. Regarding the style of the discourse, as a result, it varies between the language of retelling events and the matter-of-fact register which can be found in the reports.

Aarseth's typology Turning to the categories set up by AARSETH we can state what follows: As far as transiency is concerned, we can identify both transient and intransient characteristics within the text. Quite at the beginning, the sentence "Kokura: A Japanese city that was the primary target of the atomic bomb [...]" remains on the screen for several seconds without the reader being able to proceed by clicking a link. This is an transient feature of the text as well as the constantly looping (and unstoppable) of the technical facts concerning the nuclear tests, which are constantly present on top of the screen. The rest of the text, however, is intransient in that the reader needs to decide which link to choose in order to forward the story.

Access to the text is clearly controlled: The authors have not included a navigational item which could serve as a table-of-contents, and as a consequence, in order to reach a fragment such as man30.htm, the reader has got to click through all preceding fragments.

When analysing the way in which the authors interlink the work's fragments it follows that linking is generally explicit since the link-targets always remain the same and do not alter depending on the respective situation. However, this statement needs to be

---

[41] http://www.eastgate.com/Kokura/found/found2.htm, accessed 25.04.05

6. Analysis

qualified because the actual textual fragments that carry the link in each of the three strands, i.e. the binary sequences, remain unchanged throughout the text. Seen from this perspective, they are also conditional, because depending which fragment the reader reads, the same binary sequence leads to a different fragment each time.

Suter's typology Basically, the present text can be read in two ways: it is either possible to read each textual strand from the beginning to the end. When seen from this perspective, taking into consideration the three different textual strands, it is possible to apply the label 'tentacle' here. At a very early stage, the reader decides which of the three nodes he would like to choose, and he can consequently read all the remaining modules in a quasi-linear manner until he has reached the final one. However, it is also possible to substantiate the claim that *kokura* is a rhizome: Potentially, after having entered the text, the reader can browse the text endlessly, because the links that enable the reader to jump between the strands are always present. As a consequence, the reading of the text never comes to a real ending, which is indicative for the rhizomatic structure.

6.6. ****[four stars]

⇒   Author: Michael ATAVAR

⇒   Award: trAce/Alt-X Hypertext Competition 1998 Honourable Mention

General description and technology   The present work has been produced over a period of 12 months, which is also very obvious from its internal structure. Michael ATAVAR provides the reader with a step-by-step procedure in order to reach personal happiness and freedom. The reason for including it in our corpus of primary texts was mainly that the author experiments with the dimensions of the visible area of his work on the computer-screen.

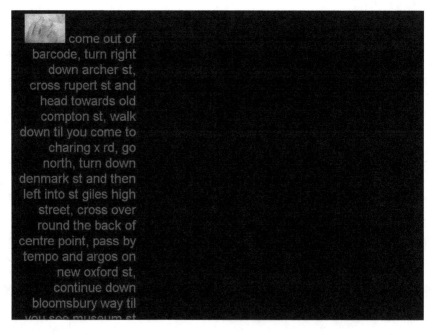

Figure 6.6.

" **** [four stars]"

Navigation and linking The initial screen features four graphical representations of a star, each one containing a link. On closer inspection it becomes evident that each of the four links leads to the same page. This second index contains the names of all months, starting from January, a fact which underlines the work's origin as 'writing on the go'. Strikingly, the single words are arranged successively on a horizontal axis, making it hence necessary for the reader to use the horizontal scroll-bar of the browser in order to be able to access all the links. Usually, in (non-fictional, i.e. purely informational) webdesign it is a major flaw in the conceptualisation and programming of a website to force readers to scroll horizontally, because it disproportionately increases the effort to locate the desired information. Seen from the artistic point of view, the chosen structure thus undermines widely-accepted conventions in order to gain a specific artistic effect.

This principle is maintained when the reader clicks on the word "February" and the following sentence appears, which contains no line-breaks:

> 1) make a list of everything that you own 2) all the small things that you might have overlooked - keys bills rubbers books (don't forget the back issues of honcho and the cheap pink ring) 3) then finally miraculously put them back - leave, lock the door to your house and walk out far away into the sunlight and breathe[42]

Here, the author uses the structure of a list to realise this fragment, which in itself requires a vertical itemisation. In other words, the structural irregularity is even more foregrounded with regard to this example. As to the artistic effect this example achieves, we can say that by scrolling from left to right, the monitor only reveals one word at a time, encouraging the reader to pay closer attention to every new word that appears on the right side of the screen. If a text is displayed on the screen, the reader can grasp the extent of it in one view, however, here, this is not possible. Similarly, artistic play with the viewable area of the screen is also reflected in another fragment (cf. figure 6.6). The written text of this module reads:

come out of

---

[42]http://www.atavar.com/fourstars/february/februarystart.html, accessed 25.04.05

> barcode, turn right
>
> down archer st,
>
> cross rupert st and
>
> head towards old
>
> compton st, walk
>
> [43]

The written text spans not more than 20 % of the screen, the other portion is only an empty space with a black background, thus again forcing the reader to scroll down and read line by line. Although this fragment is a narrative text, the way in which it is presented graphically on screen reminds us of the way in which poets purposefully arrange their poems.

As far as the interlinking of the text-fragments is concerned, the present work offers very little to the reader. In fact, when the reader has finished reading the fragment(s) belonging to the individual months that serve as access-points, he has to repeatedly click the browser's back-button in order to go back to the initial main-navigation to enter another strand. In doing so, the author forces the reader to reread the series of fragments in reverse order; in effect, therefore, we can say that the lack of links or other omnipresent navigational items adds another textual layer to the piece of hyperfiction. In the present work this is especially obvious in the "sky"[44] fragments: Here, the reader merely sees about thirty yellow or blue stars respectively on a black surface. Each star represents a link that leads to a new lexia containing a man's name and a back-arrow which enables the reader to click back to the collection of stars. If one examines every link and comes back to the main screen every time, this has considerable implications for the ensuing reading: the reader has got to click the back-button more than sixty times in order to come back, revisiting all the names in reverse order.

---

[43]`http://www.atavar.com/fourstars/april/aprilstart.html`, accessed 25.04.05

[44]`http://www.atavar.com/fourstars/january/januarystart.html`,   `http://www.atavar.com/`
`fourstars/december/decembermap.html`, accessed 25.04.05

Narrative   Regarding the narrative of ****, I suggest that it will not yield quite as relevant results because of the way the author has arranged his lexias. The narrative features a narrator who addresses the audience directly by giving them direct "instructions". At the same time, however, he seems to be 'within' the story, making him a homodiegetic narrator who does what he has ordered the reader to do. An inventory of all the narrator's personal belongings is given when clicking on the word "breathe" in the extract given above. Hence, the narrator answers himself in this case, giving an example of what the reader should do at the same time.

Aarseth's typology   Following the characteristics set up by AARSETH I suggest to classify the present work as being determinable. As with most of the works which have been discussed before, the internal cause-and-effect sequence of the individual lexia is not altered. Furthermore, this piece of hyperfiction bears all characteristics of intransiency because the user needs to click on the links in order to forward the narrative constantly (even if this involves repeatedly clicking the back-button of the browser as seen above). Access to the text is mostly controlled, although the initial subdivision into twelve main-points allows for a small degree of randomness with regard to reading-order. Finally, linking is explicit, there is no randomising function involved which would vary the link target in this piece of hyperfiction.

Suter's typology   I suggest that the present work is organised in a tentacle-structure. After having decided which of the months to choose, the reader follows down the path until the very last fragment, which at the same time constitutes a dead end. In order to go back to the main-navigation and follow another tentacle, the reader needs to click the back-button of his browser to reach the starting-point, and during this process he reads the lexias of the respective tentacle in reverse order.

6.7. *water always writes in *plural

⇒ Authors: Linda CARROLI, Josephine WILSON

⇒ Award: trAce/Alt-X Hypertext Competition 1998 Honourable Mention

General description and technology   The present work is mainly characterised by the authors' intention to experiment with the concept of metafictionality - according to SHUMATE, "[W]hile it is certainly about fiction and teases us with elements of fiction such as plot and suspense, to read it with the hope of finding a developed story is to ask to be annoyed."[45] Starting from the initial sentence "a woman stands on a streetcorner waiting for a stranger", the reader is free to explore the half fictional half-metafictional text. The ensuing text is slightly reminiscent of BECKETT's *Waiting for Godot* in that a character is waiting for someone or something without knowing who or what exactly it is. Oscillating between fiction and non-fiction, the present text circles around the concept of strangers and women in public.

Regarding the background-structure and the programming which underlies the work, I would like to draw attention to the fact that the authors present their work in standard HTML-programming without elaborate frame-structures or audio- and video-sequences. The only thing that is striking about the graphics which are used is the fact that written text is "graphicalised", which will be further discussed in the paragraph on the hypertextual characteristics of *water always writes in *plural.

Navigation and linking   On the splash-screen the reader can read - before a graphical background resembling water or something liquid in general - the title of the work as well as references concerning the authors and the supporting institutions. After clicking the work's title, the reader is transported to what could be called the main navigation consisting of the sentence "a woman stands on a street corner waiting for a stranger". This sentence consist of four fragments, a closer inspection of which will be performed in the next paragraph. When you click the word "woman" for example, a fragment

---

[45]http://www.duke.edu/~mshumate/hyperizons/original/winners1.html, accessed 25.04.05

---

a woman

stands on a
street corner

waiting

for a stranger

An online collaboration by

Linda Carroli + Josephine Wilson

Figure 6.7.

*" *water always writes in *plural"*

containing quite a large text - in comparison to the ones we have analysed so far - appears, the initial paragraph of which reads like:

> This is of course, from the point of view of the woman, an impossible story.
>
> Can you wait for a completely empty signifier? There is something this woman is not telling us. Or, there must be a third party who has told this woman 'Wait on that corner and you will see a stranger.' (And this then must be a town where there is only one stranger; this must be the day 'the stranger came to town').
>
> Or else, to jump the frame, there must be a narrator, who is not waiting but is instead withholding [...][46]

As a whole, the present fragments resembles a (printed) academic treatise more than a fragment belonging to a fictional text, containing quotations by critics such as BARTHES and DERRIDA the sources of which are indicated by means of footnotes.

The connection between link and link-target resembles that of the trope of synecdoche: The word "waiting", for instance, leads the reader to a comprehensive discussion of the various aspects of "waiting", which is - quite fittingly - also titled "on waiting":

---

[46]http://www.hypertxt.com/sh/hyper98/water/water/woman.html, accessed 25.04.05

A woman stands on a street corner waiting for a stranger

This is of course, from the point of view of the woman, an impossible story.

Can you wait for a completely empty signifier?
There is something this woman is not telling us. Or, there must be a third party who has told this woman 'Wait on that corner and you will see a stranger.' (And this then must be a town where there is only one stranger; this must be the day 'the stranger came to town').

Or else, to jump the frame, there must be a narrator, who is not waiting but is instead withholding - one for whom 'waiting' is a ploy, a tactic, a way of making us hold our breath (Next Please!)

Our narrator knows about waiting. She knows what it does to the reader. She knows all about about women waiting on dark roads beside broken-down cars.

She knows about waiting for taxis, about rides on open roads (thumb out.) She knows that women who wait for strangers are courting danger, madness, or at least, at least sadness.

So, so here comes the feminine, straddling a chasm readers name Pathetic (having in hand their Map of Prior Readings.) There she stands, our lady in waiting, attending the return of the husband she never had, the lover who did not phone back, alone on a corner, waiting for a way out ...

Est-ce toi, chere Elise ... ~ Is that you, Elise dear ...

Figure 6.8.

" *water always writes in *plural"

In writing about waiting, I feel that I am really writing about impatience. Wait. I repeat the word to convey its manifold applications; apprehension, wait, warning, wait, restraint, wait, expectation, wait, passivity, wait, yielding, wait, doubt, wait.[47]

Moreover, links are also used in an ironical way, an extreme example of which is the link "Kindness of strangers"[48] which leads to the following record of a computer-chat between the protagonist and a stranger:

linda: hello. i just wanted to look around. see what was happening.

gamma: gamma gently takes linda in his arms and embraces her

linda: sorry love - not today

gamma: bitch, bitch, bitch bitch. you fucking bitch! scum slut bitch! cunt slag! fucking smash your brains through your fucking skull. stupid pig shit bitch. break your fucking neck. smash you. burn you, witch. break your fucking legs!! MELT YOUR SKIN WITH ACID FUCKING BITCH!!! DESTROY YOUR FUCKING

---

[47]http://www.hypertxt.com/sh/hyper98/water/water/Waiting.html, accessed 25.04.05
[48]http://www.hypertxt.com/sh/hyper98/water/water/quiet.html, accessed 25.04.05

CUNT!! FUCKING MAGGOT QUEEN!!⁴⁹

Thus, here we have a rather extreme case of the functions of links being subverted by the author: The word 'kindness' could not have found a more unkind manifestation.

Generally speaking, it can be said that the present work does not provide the reader with an elaborate menu-structure, but rather uses the four different fragments provided by the initial sentence as access points for the discourse.

Hypertextual characteristics The work almost exclusively consists of written text. However, despite the lack of graphical images, the letters, words and sentences that *water* is made of carry graphical characteristics and implications themselves.

Technically speaking, "a woman stands on a street corner waiting for a stranger" is not programmed as written text but rather consists of four individual images carrying parts of the text ("a woman" - "stands on a streetcorner" - "waiting" - "for a stranger"). In doing so, the authors can take advantage of the fact that they are now in full control of the way in which the text appears on the screen of the readers. As has been discussed previously in Chapter 4, the usage of font-faces and -sizes is always problematic because each text might be displayed differently according to which technical set-up the respective reader uses. As a result of the "graphicalisation" of the written text, the four images are set in entirely different colours and faces.

The principle of graphically shaping certain parts of the written text is maintained throughout the text, thus enabling the authors to draw the reader's attention to specific parts of it. If they had done it otherwise, i.e. presenting the text in long columns in black-and-white, using the same font-type and font-size throughout, the text would have lost its hypertextual "feel" and would have looked more like a scanned in - thus digitised - version of a text already existing in print. Therefore, I suggest that by using a heterogenous layout of the written text, the fragmentisation of the hypertext is increased, or in other words, the lexias are even more fragmented using this technique.

---

⁴⁹`http://www.hypertxt.com/sh/hyper98/water/water/kill.html`, accessed 25.04.05

Furthermore, specific items of the discourse are highlighted, for instance the various alterations of the narrative point of view. In `worry.html` (cf. Fig. 6.8) two perspectives are separated by the way they are presented on screen. The major portion of the text is organised in two columns, containing a discussion about the 'empty signifier' and its implications for the narrative. Contrasted by a different font-size and -colour, this discussion is intersected by side-comments of the I-narrator: "Or perhaps it is more simple [...]" - "Don't worry, it may never happen. That's what I'm worried about ..." Another useful application of this principle is the separation of fictional and nonfictional text. As most of the hypertext consists of metafictional and quasi-academic reflections on the kind of text that is presented to the reader, it seems necessary to separate the quotations and the sources from the rest of the text. Here, the authors employ a formatting quite similar to that of academic printed texts: Quotations are written in italics and indented, and the sources are written in footnotes at the bottom of the page.

On the subject of interactivity it needs to be noted that the user-participation is of a lesser degree than regarding *The Unknown* or *These Waves of Girls*. We can identify several reasons for this state of affairs: First of all, the lack of transient items, i.e. sound- or video-files which are being played without the user having the possibility to influence their progression, decreases interactivity. Also, individual fragments are comparably long and in many cases bear all characteristics of academic treatises, as has been previously discussed. And finally, there are quite a number of fragments which, despite of their length, contain only one or two links, further reducing the reader's options.[50]

The degree of interactivity also directly influences the question of the work's linearity. On the intrafragmental level, the work can clearly be identified as being 'mono-sequential' in that the internet as the method of publication does not influence the text as all. Most fragments could actually be transferred into their paper-form without losing too much of their usability or readability, i.e. they are very close to their printed counterparts. As regards the interfragmental level, however, the text becomes multi-

---

[50]Cf. `http://www.hypertxt.com/sh/hyper98/water/water/quiet.html` or `http://www.hypertxt.com/sh/hyper98/water/water/laughter.html`, accessed 25.04.05

sequential and leaves the reading-path up to the reader.

Arguably, the most prominent hypertextual feature that can be identified regarding *water always writes in *plural* is the degree of intertextuality the authors employ in their work. The academic discourse - involving theorists such as DERRIDA and writers like THOREAU is by far more complex and developed than the initial fictional setting of the work. In *kokura*, the work we have analysed before, the fictional narrative was embedded in the non-fictional news-reports which provided social and political reference. Referring to the present work, however, this relationship has been turned upside down, and the main emphasis lies on the non-fictional part.

Similarly to all the works we have examined so far, the authors equip their work with a splash-screen containing all relevant bibliographical data. As with most of the other works this presentation is dealing with, by using this method authors use conventions of traditional printed literature in order to add stability and identifiability to their piece of hyperfiction. The work itself, for this reason, is characterised by a closed structure, even though the text-borders are in danger to become blurred by the extensive use of related secondary material.

Seen from the reception-side of the communication-process, I suggest that because of the work's linear structure and its clear relationship between link and link-target, the construction of coherent readings is facilitated, despite the fact that the narrative is not centered around its fictional basis but rather turns the nonfictional elements into a metanarrative.

Narrative Concerning the story-level of the present narrative, I would first of all like to refer to the events which are described in this work. As has been discussed before, the work mostly consists of secondary material on the topics of waiting, boredom, and the "manners of ladies". Hence, it does not come as a surprise to find that there are hardly any events at all. We are presented with an initial scene in which the woman is waiting for a stranger, and a rather long fragment which describes a phone-call the woman makes, talking to a stranger in Germany. These events are only slightly related and rather stress the woman's wish to get to know a man - and eventually - her husband:

> She finds husbands everywhere - in counters behind delis, under the watchful eyes of wives and girlfriends. On street corners, at bus stops, stepping out of cars in petrol stations. They light cigarettes, sip coffee, turn over the pages of books. Too often the betrothed are joined by friends, women, and the knot is broken.[51]

These events are, however not temporally connected, and the causal connection is only established in so far as the fictional events of the narrative deal with the woman's wish to meet someone.

Parallel to this, the question of which characters appear in the story is also problematic to answer because ultimately there are only the woman and the foreign man she exchanges a couple of sentences with during their telephone conversation. Both characters are not developed by the authors at all, they seem more like "illustrative material" used to clarify the ideas and concepts that are conveyed in the secondary texts. This way of making use of the characters is also reflected in the creation of the settings. Only during the telephone-conversation do we get to know that the female protagonist is located in Northern America, and the second character in Berlin. However, the setting does not have any influence on the development of the narrative.

On the discourse-level of the narrative, the analytical problems with regard to *water always writes in *plural are also quite tangible. Since there are hardly any narrated events, the analysis on the levels of order, duration, and frequency cannot be substantiated. Regarding the latter, however, it should be noted that the link-structure of the text makes it possible for a fragment to appear more than once.

Characterisation - specifically that of the female protagonist, is mostly performed in direct mode, either by a telling description or by an theoretical text reflecting on specific character traits the woman has as well as social and gender-centered roles she has got to perform.

---

[51] http://www.hypertxt.com/sh/hyper98/water/water/Berlin.html, accessed 25.04.05

The fact that the present work is a mixture of a fictional work and an academic treatise also has some implications for the narrative situation. In the extract just quoted, the perspective of the narrator is as far detached from the story as one could imagine. Taking the point of view of a literary critic, the heterodiegetic focaliser reflects on the meaning of the initial sentence ("a woman stands on a streetcorner waiting for a stranger"), thus highlighting the metafictional potential of the text.

Regarding the fictional parts of the text, the narrative perspective is altered considerably. A good example here is the module "denouement":

There is one story I cannot exhaust.

The story of You.

I can never make *you* happy.

But what about them - can I make*them* [sic] happy?[52]

The third-person-narration becomes an I-narration here. In other words, it can be argued that here we can also witness a shift from a heterodiegetic to a homodiegetic narrator, since this statement could stem from the woman herself.

The narrator refers to the audience as *them* and offers three different endings to the story - "But what are the options? One two three."[53] Here, by clicking on one of the three links, the reader is able to access three solutions to the narrative.

The first option again features another point of view, namely the one of the metafictional critic: "[...] There is a killer out there, waiting for women who stand on street corners. In this scenario, the one we know well, waiting is catastrophic."[54]

Secondly, the author offers a happy ending:

A stranger stops, asks the woman on the corner the time. "At the third stroke"

she replies, "it will be 4.55 and 20 seconds". He smiles, laughs, thank you! Coffee?

---

[52]http://www.hypertxt.com/sh/hyper98/water/water/you.html, accessed 25.04.05

[53]http://www.hypertxt.com/sh/hyper98/water/water/you.html, 25.04.05

[54]http://www.hypertxt.com/sh/hyper98/water/water/one.html, accessed 25.04.05

You know what it is? It is of course, electricity. A Love Switch. Live wire, heat,

conduction. [...][55]

The last option features another woman:

A stranger approaches, asks our Lady-in-Waiting the way to a small hidden garden

that opens only one day of the year - this day, this year - a garden few know about,

fewer care about, and even less visit.

I will show you, our woman says, taken by the frank smile of the stranger, and her

rather fabulous black wool coat which bears a strong resemblance to that worn by

Lana Turner in a movie she saw long ago.

She has style, this stranger.[56]

The present text can be referred to as being multi-modal because of its hybrid fictional-

non-fictional structure. Similarly, it also contains multiple styles, namely that of aca-

demic discourse and that of a fictional description of the woman's situation.

Aarseth's typology   Analysed in view of the respective categories developed by AAR-

SETH, the present text can be classified as follows: The work's internal structure does

not contain any random elements as we have seen in the discussion above. In other

words, as far as determinability is concerned we can label it 'determinable': clicking on

a respective link always leads to the same results, so the traversal function is stable.

Furthermore, as far as the development of the story is concerned, it is not possible to

find any instance in the text where it is being forwarded automatically. Hence, the work

is intransient in that the reader is always required to interact with the text in order to

forward the discourse and develop a reading.

Text access is mostly controlled. Although the splash screen containing the core

sentence could be seen as a miniature table-of-contents in that it allows the reader to

randomly chose from four different beginnings, the majority of the text's fragments

remain invisible and disconnected from the start. Hence, it is necessary for the reader

---

[55]http://www.hypertxt.com/sh/hyper98/water/water/two.html, accessed 25.04.05

[56]http://www.hypertxt.com/sh/hyper98/water/water/three.html, accessed 25.04.05

to enter the text and explore the inserted links in order to browse all the fragments, i.e. text access is controlled.

Finally, following the discussion above, the interlinking of the hypertext's lexias is explicit and thereby predictable in that all links are present at all times rather than requiring a special reading path for the reader to see them.

Suter's typology The organisational principle of **water always writes in *plural* is clearly that of a rhizome: having entered the text once, potentially the reader browses the network endlessly. However, the authors undermine this endlessness by providing a conscious ending to the story. When we talked about the way in which navigation is supported and encouraged by the text, we were confronted with a fragment called "denouement", in which the authors offer three different ways of terminating the discourse. From the literary point of view, the text contains a sense of closure which is however not supported by the work's overall structure. The reader - in theory - can choose the ending and conclude his reading because the final fragments clearly deliver a solution to the plot. However, even in the very last fragment the authors have placed a link that takes the reader back to the very beginning.

This discussion shows that in order to be able to give a justified evaluation of a hyperfictional work's internal structure, one needs to consider both overall structuring and the content of the individual fragments.

6.8. IN MEMORY DO WE TRUST?

⇒ Author(s): DLSAN

General description and technology I have chosen this work because regarding both form and content it is quite different from all the other texts we have examined so far. Here, the author 'clones' the official tourist-information website of the city of Verona in Italy and - in quite a subtle way - adds alternative images and texts to the site, which are full of piercing irony. In other words, the author creates a parody of a well-known genre, namely the informational website, and thus creates a work which features both characteristics of a fictional and of a non-fictional text.

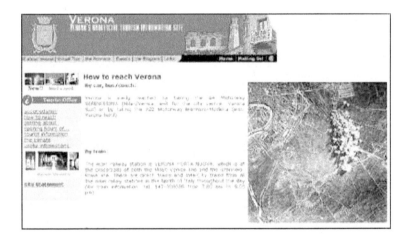

Figure 6.9.

"IN MEMORY DO WE TRUST?"

Usually, these websites are not fictitious and aim at informing the visitor about a company and/or a product. Here, however, the author has subtly manipulated the site in such a way that it fits into the context of war criticism: using a website which was originally intended to let the city of Verona appear in the best possible light in order to attract tourists, he completely reverses the meaning and creates a context of horror and death.

A question which needs to be addressed here, naturally, is whether the present work is really a narrative. I propose that this is only the case as far as the intertextual implications are concerned. The parody refers to the overall concept of war, some scenes of which are employed in the text via photographs. In other words, this project can be seen as belonging to the general WW2-narrative. It is 'narrationsinduzierend' in that one could imagine events and characters which are only hinted at by this website-parody. Nevertheless, I think that the analysis of this work will provide a valuable discussion of the genre of websites in general and the conventional framework that they are constructed in.

IN MEMORY DO WE TRUST? was published in the context of a project that immediately caught my attention when I was searching for primary material: *wartime project*[57]. On its introductory page, it claims to include "[...] over fifty artists, individuals or groups, organizing through the internet, have contributed pieces meditating on, reflecting on and reacting against wars, past, present and future [...]".

Navigation and linking This piece of hyperfiction reaches its target because it successfully undermines and deconstructs the respective genre-expectations, in this case of an informational website. The page the user sees has been designed following these conventions, including a horizontal navigational bar with the crest of Verona and some images of the city on the top of the screen, a vertical navigation at the left-hand side, and a main window containing the content of this website. Hence, at first sight, the work does not contain any 'surprises', and it is only when the reader starts to interact with this website that he realises the ironic facets the author has included.

For instance, via the keyword "accommodation" the user is referred to a site titled "accommodation for young people"; what can be seen, however, is a grainy black-and-

---

[57]http://offline.area3.net/wartime/

white picture of two children in the middle of debris and ashes. The link "how to get there" takes the reader to a lexia which lists all the different ways of getting to the city; however, this is referred to with an ironic undertone by the fact that next to the official-sounding route-description, there is an aerial picture taken from the city, with an explosion and a cloud of dust in the middle of it.

Moreover, all graphical items used to structure the website's content, which are coloured in the original document, turn to black-and-white when the mouse-pointer touches them. Even the function for sending an e-card[58] is artistically manipulated by the author: Rather than enabling the user to send attractive photographs of Verona to the desired recipients, the images are also exchanged for black-and-white war-footage. This implies that the horror presented by the website is not only restricted to the actual visitor but can also be spread further and affect readers who have not yet accessed the page.

Likewise, the rest of the project is created this way, the sober-sounding texts are thwarted by the images that surround them, thus giving the overall site quite a different meaning.

Hypertextual characteristics   What is remarkable in this work is the way cross-mediality is used. The original webpage has used a balanced mix of written text and images in order to convey information to potential visitors to the city of Verona. As far as the occurring image-text relationships (cf. Chapter 3.4.1) are concerned, the images on the one hand totally undermine what the written text contains on the other hand. While the portions of written text live up to genre expectations of a website, the use of black-and-white-imagery, which negates what is being said and is only visible at second glance mark these as ironic - or even sarcastic - image-text relationships.

The fact that the present work is meant to be a parody of a website also implies that the usual conventions of navigation are copied. Programmers of contemporary websites

---

[58]As a special service and a promotional tool at the same time, many modern websites offer the possibility to send a so-called e-card by choosing an image, adding one's own personalised text to it and send it to a specified recipient.

constantly improve the ways in which the users can interact with the programmed structure, aiming at facilitating the quick retrieval of information as much as possible. *IN
MEMORY DO WE TRUST?* naturally inherits these characteristics and offers a very
effective and interactive interface. This structure goes hand-in-hand with the work's
nonlinearity - informational websites are *per definitionem* multisequential.

As to the overall effect of the work, the author integrates other texts into his own. The
genre-expectation he plays with can also be explained by the fact that he contextualises
his work by means of accepted standards and conventions. Moreover, by including
additional material, i.e. written text, graphics, and sound, he reinforces the work's
intertextuality.[59]

Furthermore, the present work also inherits the main characteristics of the production-
process of a website. Its referentiability and stability is ensured by the recognisable
text-borders, and the user is able to create coherent readings.

Aarseth's typology This work is determinate since regardless of the situation, the links
that are being activated always lead to exactly the same results. Regarding transiency,
I suggest that the present work is intransient: The reader, as in all other works that we
have looked at so far, has to actively participate and forward the reading experience by
selecting the respective links. Furthermore, as this work is very much influenced by the
conventions of an informational website, access is random. One criterion of a successful
website is that the respective information is available simply and quickly to respond to
the users' needs. Linking is explicit, there are no changes of the way a link appears or
reacts depending on the progress of an individual reading.

Suter's typology As for its overall structure, I believe it justified to argue that we
are dealing with a hierarchical structure here. Since *IN MEMORY DO WE TRUST?*
satirises an original web-page, but 'defaces' it in a special way, this relationship is more
than clear. The user is presented with a very clear structure enabling him to directly

---

[59]The references to the sources that are used can be accessed when clicking "Site Statement".

access all the individual branches from the main navigation. Interconnection between these individual branches is not present, so that this seems to be a very clear case indeed.

6.9. Grammatron

⇒ Author: Mark AMERIKA

⇒ ELO category: Hypertext fiction

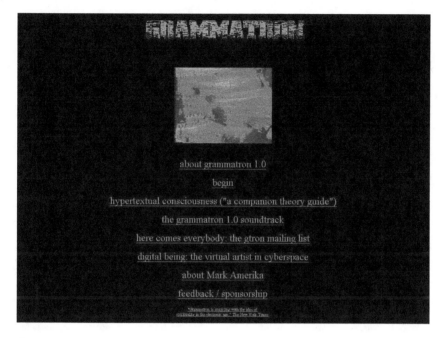

Figure 6.10.

"Grammatron"

General description and technology

In dieser Hypertextfiktion geht es um Abe Golam, genialer Poet vertrackter Text-
strings, der aus dem 21. Jahrhundert auf die Zeit zurückblickt, als diese Art von
herausgespuckter transmedialer Word-Art-Hypertext-Fiction erfunden wurde, in
die späten neunziger Jahre, in die Hochphase des WWW-Booms. [19]

This project can be said to be one of the first comprehensive works of hyperfiction
having been published on the internet, its origins, according to the author, lying in a

"[...] MS Word document that [...] was created on April 3, 1993." [79]. As regards the underlying technology of *Grammatron*, AMERIKA himself informs us:

> The project consists of over over [sic] 1100 text spaces, 2000 links, 40+ minutes of original soundtrack delivered via Real Audio 3.0, unique hyperlink structures by way of specially-coded Javascripts, a virtual gallery featuring scores of animated and still life images, and more storyworld development than any other narrative created exclusively for the Web.[60]

The work in its overall structure resembles the sort of hyperfiction that is published on CD-ROM by American publisher EASTGATE. The individual fragments, which are numerous and highly interconnected, mostly consist of only one or two sentences, which is the same organisational principle as *afternoon, a story* by Michael JOYCE [11] and *Victory Garden* by Stuart MOULTHROP [15]. Therefore, it does not come as a surprise to learn that Grammatron has been written using EASTGATE's *Storyspace*-software.[61]

Navigation and linking Linking is in fact the most striking feature of *Grammatron* since there are no navigational items other than the textual links themselves. As a result, the user might in many cases experience a sense of getting lost in hyperspace. The only item that gives the reader a sense of how much he has mastered already is the fact that the browser colours the visited links differently, and thus the more fragments one has visited, the more violet links appear in the lexias. Apart from this, however, the user has no indication of where he is located in the network - a suitable example of a rhizomatic structure. In *The Unknown*, the reader is always given the chance of turning back to a main category, or being helped by the extensive table-of-contents. In the present text, however, these features are not present at all, which makes it far more challenging - and exhausting - to read.

The initial screen shows the title of the work as well as a small animation shifting between what seems to be a person in front of a computer screen and a bit of text.

---

[60]http://www.grammatron.com/about.html, accessed 25.04.05

[61]Cf. http://www.eastgate.com/storyspace/writing/Amerika.html, accessed 25.04.05

6. Analysis

After waiting for about ten seconds or clicking the animation, the user is automatically forwarded to a second page, which also features some text links forming the basic way of browsing through *Grammatron*. These are:

about grammatron 1.0

begin

hypertextual consciousness ("a companion theory guide")

the grammatron 1.0 soundtrack

here comes everybody: the gtron mailing list

digital being: the virtual artist in cyberspace

about Mark Amerika

feedback / sponsorship

Following the link "hypertextual consciousness ("a companion theory guide")", the reader accesses a website which allows him to read a theoretical treatise on the concept of hypertext, thus yet again, the fictional work is very closely related to its self-explanatory and non-fictional counterpart. Furthermore, a link to join the *Grammatron*-mailinglist emphasises the author's intention to highlight the fact that the work itself is in a constant flux, and the readers have got the possibility to be updated about new features on a regular basis. Thus, this aspect foregrounds how a virtual community is being created, the members of which share the same interest in the present work. This, in fact, is one of the major strengths of the internet.

The narrative itself can be entered - as could have been expected beforehand - by using the link "begin". After having decided between a low and a high bandwidth version, the reader begins reading.

Hypertextual characteristics Mark AMERIKA has used a range of different cross-medial items in order to develop his piece of hyperfiction. They occur right from the beginning when the initial lexia of "interfacing" lexias are being forwarded automatically: A machine-like distorted voice together with a hypnotic droning sound in low key accompanies the fragments which themselves contain animated images. In contrast to *IN MEMORY DO WE TRUST?* which we have discussed before, the image-text and sound-text relationships are always used in additive combination (cf. Chapter 3.4.1), i.e. they support each other in order to heighten the artistic effect.

Regarding the concepts of interactivity and non-linearity, after having chosen the initial link "interfacing" in order to begin reading *Grammatron*, the reader is presented with approximately 80 lexias which are being switched automatically by the underlying programmed script. Thus, he is not given any possibility to interact with the text, but rather needs to read and watch the succession of fragments passively. According to WENZ [88], however, this stylistic device bears certain problems:

> Typisch für Hypertext ist allerdings - trotz der vor allem geschriebenen Texte im Web - ein Verhalten, wie wir es im Umgang mit anderen visuellen Medien geübt haben: nämlich zapping, channel switching. Das erzwungene Lesen führt bei den meisten Rezipienten bereits an dieser Stelle zu einem Abbruch der Lektüre, wie Mark Amerika nach einem Versuch mit Studenten erkannte, und nicht wie erhofft zu einem verstärkten Bewußtsein des eigenen Mediengebrauchs und der daran geknüpften Erwartungen.

The structure of these initial fragments, hence, is mono-sequential in that no possibility is being offered to diverge from the path the author has laid out before. However, this structure is altered after the initial "film" has come to an end and the reader accessed the first lexia titled "Abe Golam".[62] Here, user interaction is required in order to forward the text, and at this point the reader is "[...] hineingezogen in den Sog einer insgesamt tausend Bildschirmseiten umfassenden Welt aus Bildern, Texten und Tönen." [58]

Quite importantly for the development of the narrative in *Grammatron*, the author refers to the writing of the Cabala ("[...] source-code that suggests letters create words

---

[62]It is also possible to skip the introductory sequence by selecting "Abe Golam" directly from the main-menu of the very first page.

create consciousness create Man [...]" [42] as well as the Jewish myth of the "Golem":

> In many way GTRON is a virtual remake of the Golem myth that expresses how life
> itself is born by way of marking letters on the body. But of course in GTRON the
> lead-avatar figure, Abe Golam, is an electronic disembodiment, and this enables
> me to play around with Jewish mysticism in new ways [..] [42]

In other words, the author uses an altered version of a known myth as the basic
setting for his work. Intertextuality, thus, is not integrated by means of links which in
a suggestive way connect to surrounding texts in order to achieve the desired artistic
effect. Rather, the narrative *itself* draws on these texts.

Narrative The first fragment the reader encounters already prepares the ground for
those which are to follow, because the individual modules are quite similar as far as
their arrangement on screen is concerned. What the reader sees is a couple of lines of
text, many words of which are coloured blue, a clear indicator of links. Furthermore, the
background image features a somewhat blurred grey text on a white surface; the only
words which can be clearly identified here are "worthless" and "worries", so the first
impression is one of pessimism and tension, which is quite different from the atmosphere
created by the author of *These Waves of Girls*, as we have seen in our previous analysis.
The third item visible on screen is a small grainy animation of a face, which oscillates
between two states of movement.

The written text introduces us to the main character of the narrative we have also
met in the metafictional section of *Grammatron* before. Abe Golam, as he is named, is
described in the following way:

> Abe Golam, legendary info-shaman, cracker of the sorcerer-code and creator of
> Grammatron and Nanoscript, sat behind his computer, every speck of creative
> ore long since excavated from his burnt-out brain, wondering how he was going to
> survive in the electrosphere he had once called home.[63]

---

[63]http://www.grammatron.com/gtronbeta/Abe_Golam_907.html, accessed 25.04.05

6. Analysis

Thus, in the present case, all the items - and here I refer to both the graphical and the written text - contribute to the same overall tone, and according to McCloud's elaborations on text-image relationship, we can without a doubt suggest that here we have a case where all elements support each other. The narrative develops by Abe Golam describing his alternate persona, the grammatron, which is "[...] a genderless prognosticator of electronic riffs spreading itself throughout the electrosphere. [...]"[64]. Another important element of the plot is "Nanoscript", the language of the *Grammatron*. The narrative unfolds by the reader clicking the links and being transported to other lexias, however, the connection between the word that is being touched and the new text that is being opened as a consequence bears almost no tangible connection. This is quite different from *The Unknown* for example, where the links and their 'counterparts' intuitively 'made sense'. With regard to the present text, however, this idea is starkly undermined in some instances:

> Now you see it now you don't. <u>Writing comes</u>, writing goes. IT comes: meanwhile, there goes the creature. Flux. Link. Peak. Reboot? Ignore? Abort?"[65]

The link which is underlined in the citation above leads to the following fragment:

> Oh oh oh oh oh oh oh oh oh oh oh oh oh oh...[66]

This example, in fact, very clearly illustrates two phenomena: For one, the connection between the link and the target in this case is a very loose one, it is not recognisable at first sight why the author has chosen to link the phrase. [67] Also, the narrative value of a hypertext-fragment can almost be zero, as is the case with "oh oh oh [...]". For this reason it comes as a surprise that despite its narrative triviality, the fragment serves as an important navigational item as it serves as entry-point to another story-line - in

---

[64] `http://www.grammatron.com/gtronbeta/Genderless_818.html`, accessed 25.04.05

[65] `http://www.grammatron.com/gtronbeta/abort_200.html`, accessed 25.04.05

[66] `http://www.grammatron.com/gtronbeta/Oh_076.html`, accessed 25.04.05

[67] Taking into consideration the sexual overtones in some of the fragments, it could be possible to suggest that the author has referred to the slang-meaning of 'writing comes' (writing has an orgasm), and therefore he offers the "oh oh oh [...]"-fragment as the link target.

other words, each of the fourteen "oh's" is a link taking the reader to totally different parts of the plot. This proves how it is crucial to both take a look at the background and the surface structure, especially with regard to links.

The setting is the bizarre and futuristic "Prague-23" referred to as "Cyburbia"[68], which is mainly characterised by the way in which especially the main character only communicates with the real word via the computer, and vice versa. Also, the characters only seem to exist in cyberspace:

> At this point a virtual babe with cosmic cleave and digital dew-drops dripping off
> her pseudo-collagen inflamed lips started deep tonguing the screen coming at all
> the viewers as if she were ready to lick the radiation right off their dour faces [...][69]

The only real character apart from the protagonist is his former lover Cynthia, who, being a programmer herself ("Cynthia's programming skills and technical aesthetic were beyond brilliant."[70]) has left Golam. Within the more than 1200 fragments *Grammatron* consists of, the search for Cynthia is described. She is described as being his "second half", and the reunion with her also means the completion of the digital being 'Grammatron' they have programmed together (cf. SHAVIRO [77]).

The discourse is marked by the achronous ordering of events and the frequent shifts of perspective, style and narrative mode. Generally speaking, *Grammatron* is told by an authorial narrator who constantly switches between the descriptions of Abe and Cynthia.

Furthermore, there are instances of communication which in language as well as in graphical realisation on screen resemble memos or emails. This use of different text types, intersected by graphical images which do not forward the actual plot - they are mostly advertisements for virtual sex - contribute to the highly fragmented character of *Grammatron*.

---

[68]http://www.grammatron.com/gtronbeta/cyburbia_266.html, accessed 25.04.05

[69]http://www.grammatron.com/gtronbeta/babe_254.html, accessed 25.04.05

[70]http://www.grammatron.com/gtronbeta/kitchen3_670.html, accessed 25.04.05

Aarseth's typology Regarding the internal cause-and-effect relationship of the links respectively lexias in this work we can state that they are determinable. As far as transiency is concerned, we can attribute both intransient and transient since *Grammatron* does not unfold itself without the users' participation in some parts. In the cases where a soundfile or a piece of animation is integrated, the user is always given the possibility to click further. However, the initial automatic sequence resembles a film and is therefore a transient feature. Because of its structure, the access to the narrative is very controlled and limited. The user enters the text once and then encounters new fragments on the way, without the ability to specifically select one individual module right from the start which is actually located "deeper" in the hypertextual structure. Linking is explicit because there is no random function included which influences the way in which the links are connected to the targets they aim at.

Suter's typology *Grammatron* is a good example of a rhizomatic structure, the striking feature of the text is its complexity and the high degree of interlinking. Once the reader has entered the narrative, he can move around in it almost endlessly. The individual fragments are not hierarchically ordered in any recognisable sense, so the reader is required to explore the network and read the fragments in random order. Of course, this also implies that several fragments can be visited more than once in a reading session, and the session itself only finds an end when the reader "has had enough". There are also instances of linearity to be found in the hypertext structure: some lexias contain only one link which connects them to the subsequent ones, reducing the user-interaction and letting the reader experience an almost linear succession of events the author has laid out before.

6.10. Rice

⇒ Author: GENIWATE

⇒ Award: trAce/Alt-X Hypertext Competition 1998 1st Prize

⇒ ELO category: Hypertext poetry

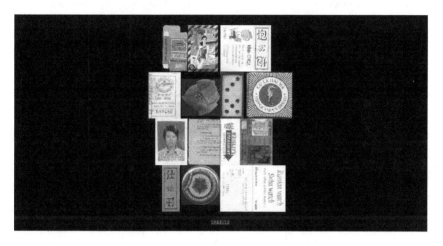

Figure 6.11.

"Rice"

General description and technology The various small poems and video-fragments mostly deal with the history of Vietnam and the situation of the country today, being looked at from the perspective of an Australian tourist, thus we can assume that this work is at least partly autobiographical because the author is an Australian. On the initial screen the reader is presented with technical information as to which programmes (or versions of programmes) have been used by the writer and which of these need to be installed on the reader's computer in order for the work to display properly. *Shockwave* for example is a technology developed to enable authors to make use of elaborate multi-media elements in their works.

Regarding the title of the work as well as the central issue of the work - namely *"Rice"*

- CHANG [30] argues:

> Metaphorically, the project's title itself invites interrogation – rice as a struc-
> tural principle conjures intriguing possibilities: the particular (grain-level) and
> the whole; abundance; uniformity; even a quality of random sampling that, once
> repeated often enough, leads to a greater overall understanding. It is also worth
> noting that rice, as a staple of the Asian diet and one of the stereotypical repre-
> sentations of Eastern living, connotes difference [...]

Navigation and linking   What is striking right from the start is the fact that the writer
seems to be very self-aware of the question of authorship and referentiability since on
the very first page the user is presented the following information:

> rice is best viewed using version 4 or better browser. Shockwave and frames are
> used. This project was developed during a residency at the Media Resource Centre,
> Adelaide. The project was supported by the MRC and the Australia Council, the
> Federal Government's arts funding and advisory body.
>
> Deepest thanks to Oscar Ferreiro for photos and junk [...][71]

When clicking the word "rice", the reader is being transported to the main navigation,
which consists of sixteen small images ("thumbnails") such as a chewing gum wrapping
paper and a crown cap. By clicking the small images, individual lexias can be accessed.
On this sub-level, the fragments are arranged in a circular manner: a couple of lines are
presented together with a button indicating "next", then some more lines are presented,
until finally the reader gets back to the initial navigational page.

Hypertextual characteristics   The writer makes use of the combination of photo-
graphic images and written texts. Additionally, there is also a small video-clip in
poem8.html which adds yet another layer of interpretation to the overall analysis. The
clip (which can be accessed from four different buttons) is filmed in black and white,
and shows grainy images of a map, soldiers and Vietnamese civilians. On top of that,

---

[71]http://www.idaspoetics.com.au/rice/riceheading.html, accessed 25.04.05

we hear people singing "all we are saying, is give peace a chance", President John F. Kennedy's announcement that military actions against the North-Vietnamese have begun, and a radio-broadcast in Vietnamese. In other words, this short clip of ten seconds or so presents us the American and Vietnam point of view to this conflict, and also refers to the anti-war movement in general. The use of different media in the work leads to a high degree of interactivity. As we will see in a closer analysis, the individual fragments of the work are rather short and often consist of only a couple of lines. Therefore, the reader has to make reading decisions constantly and the work has to be read at a high pace. This interactivity is only slightly reduced when the reading has used one of the few multimedia-items, which slows down the reading.

As a consequence, *Rice* is also multisequential in that the grid of sixteen images serving as the main menu can be browsed in random order and the high degree of user-participation results in fragmented and non-linear readings.

Moreover, we find yet another example of how the concept of intertextuality can be used: When clicking "CREDITS", which is located on the navigational page at the bottom of the images, it reveals references to two other written texts and a piece of music. This way of presenting bibliographical information is quite wide-spread in print, and the new electronic form of writing apparently strives for this academic correctness and quotes its sources. This, as could be argued, is more evidence that hypertext and standard printed texts are not so much different after all. The texts quoted[72] are being used in the work to give some backgrounds information about the history and the development of Vietnam. Thus, this is a good example of intertextuality. Also, the writer uses different text sorts which coexist to make up a coherent whole, another example of collage.

The present piece of hyperfiction can be regarded a closed structure because of the circular navigational arrangement and the lacking of links which would take the reader "outside" the text. Therefore, publication would also be possible on a CD-ROM for

---

[72]GARNIER, *The French in IndoChina*, T Nelson and Sons, London, 1884, Gettleman, *M.E. Vietnam - History, Documents, and Opinions on a Major World Crisis*, Penguin, London, 1966

example because it is not dependent on external links. For this reason, reception of *Rice* is also not threatened to be complicated by a rhizomatic and infinite arrangement of the lexias the work consists of, i.e. it is not problematic for the reader to construct coherent readings.

Narrative and poetry   As has already become obvious by the way in which the ELD categorises this work, we are presented with a hypertext which bears strong resemblances to poetry. Apart from this categorisation, a number of characteristics could be listed which stress the poetic qualities of *Rice*. First of all, the file-names include the word "poem" so the author - who in this sense could more suitably be described as the poet - stresses the fact that she presents her work as poetry. Also, the arrangement of the individual poems on the screen is reminiscent of traditional printed poetry.

Since this dissertation is primarily concerned with the discussion of the narratological characteristics of hyperfiction on the internet, it would be beyond our scope to specifically refer to the 'foregrounded regularity' such as phonological repetition, rhythmic parallels and verbal repetition as well as the 'foregrounded irregularity' such as lexical, grammatical or graphological deviation as proposed by WENZEL [89, p.171]. Rather, I would like to briefly refer to the narrative properties of poetry:

In her essay "Lyrik und Narratologie", MÜLLER-ZETTELMANN examines how tools from narratology such as the story-discourse dichotomy can be applied to poetic texts. She begins her argument by remarking, "[...] daß die lyrische Analysepraxis innerhalb der [...] Disziplin der modernen Literatur- und Kulturwissenschaft einen auffallend anachronistischen Weg verfolgt." [63, p.131]. The critic then continues her discussion by tracing elements of narrative in some examples and convincingly concludes:

> Zusammenfassend kann also gesagt werden, daß es sehr wohl lohnt, eine konsequente Trennung des lyrischen Textsubtrats in *histoire* vs. *discours* vorzunehmen.
>
> [63, p.136]

Consequently, regarding the question whether *Rice* should be analysed as a narrative text or as poetry, KIERNAN [53] suggests that "[...] the audience is introduced to an

interchangeable mix of prose and poetry [...]" and that, regarding the poetic characteristics, "[T]he multitudinous difference in poetic forms used creates a compositional
tension that is held in fine balance throughout the work.'"

In Nha Trang I started to vomit.
I had taken far too many photos.
They had got into my gut.

There was nothing to do but lie low.
I went to ground on a beach-head
and tried digesting small portions of local
colour.

Finally I had strength enough to continue.
At first, vision was restricted to familiar
objects -
(toothbrushes are very reassuring).

I bought postcards of happy-go-lucky
tribespeople cheerfully toothless in the
face of poverty and discrimination.

The going rate for smiles is two American
dollars.

We were much more careful with looking
from then on.[73]

A number of issues arise from this small extract. First of all, one immediately recognises that the way the poem is graphically represented on screen does not differ from

---

[73]http://www.idaspoetics.com.au/rice/poem5.html, accessed 25.04.05

the way poems are usually set on the printed page. What I have simply done is copied the extract from the monitor screen into my word-processor and printed them out. In effect, the poem on paper does not bear any traces whatsoever of the electronic medium. As a result, we can analyse it as we would any traditional printed poem.

The subject of this specific instance is the narrator's reaction to what she sees in Vietnam, and the danger of 'looking'. As far as the narrative is concerned, we indeed find a succession of events here which are related to each other causally and temporally as well as being reflected and related by a homodiegetic narrator-focaliser. This is also reflected by other lexias. Regarding the discourse-level, we find that the aspect of duration can also be found in the present work. In `poem8.html`, which has been referred to above, the poet describes the beginning of the Vietnam War, which is an obvious example of analepsis.

Another motif of *Rice* is the idea of waste: the graphic lay-out of the work is mainly based on different items of garbage. On the splash-screen it says "[...] Deepest thanks to Oscar Ferreiro for photos and junk [...]", and the small images used as main navigation also remind us of junk. In `poem9a.html` it says:

> I am learning [] to read the junk
>
> Junk doesn't do any good. [] It can leave a nasty smell.
>
> It weightens the planet [] with discarded desire.
>
> Junk is the past. [] It makes us.
>
> Small truths in the gutter [] collecting for me.

Indeed, it seems that the poet tries to reconstruct past happenings by looking at the remainders of former times. Apart from actual photographs, she also refers to this in `poem2.html`:

> Dead thong in the delta
>
> dry rice in the dirt

and when all the people turn to dust

who will sweep up?

The motif of "junk" and its collection seems to be especially suited for a hypertext because of its fragmentary nature. As in a collage, the poet can add bits and pieces to form a coherent work of hyperfiction accessible at various points of entry. As in other electronic works, it is then up to the reader to form his own reading.

Aarseth's typology   Turning to the analytical paradigm established by AARSETH, we can pinpoint a number of details which we can use to place the present text in its generical context.

The relationship between textons and scriptons is constant in that a texton cannot generate a varying number of scriptons with regard to the present work. Regarding 'determinability' we can state that the traversal function is determinable since the sequence of scriptons within the individual poems always remains the same. The only influence the reader has is to choose the sequence of the order he would like to read the poems in. Furthermore, because the reader needs to click navigational items in order to proceed with reading the text, the work can be classified to be 'intransient'. This is only slightly undermined when the reader accesses the various bits of film and sound in *Rice*, which run from beginning to end without the user being able to alter their progression.

Arguably, access to the text can be labelled both random and controlled. On the main-navigational level, access is random since the user can decide which poem to read first. Once he opts for one and clicks the respective link, however, the access is controlled and he can only follow the path that the poet has laid out. The links in the present work are used in an explicit manner: The offsets and targets of links always remain the same.

Suter's typology   Regarding the overall-structure of *Rice*, it seems justified to suggest that it is circular: The text provides sixteen points of access, with their individual branches linking back to the main navigation after about five lexias. Thus, the reception of the individual poems which branch out from the main-navigation is stable, the author/producer retains full control over her text, making the reading experience quite close to the one of a printed poem. Also, the individual branches are not connected by links, thus the connection is purely established by the subject of the work itself. Hence, we can also see a variation of the tree-structure here.

Summary   This work is a good example of how the writing of hypertexts is of experimental character since interestingly, all the poems - technically speaking - are arranged in different ways. We are in fact dealing with what could be called a modern "collage", combining various fragments to form an artistic whole. Poems 1, 2 and 5, from their textual layout, are presented on screen as they also would be on paper, there is a characteristic splitting-up of lines. Poem 3 contains a shockwave-file which is opened in a little window and contains a series of subsequent frames which contain the text. Poem 4 uses different text-colors, in poem 6 the text scrolls from bottom to top in the centre of the screen. Also, the fact that the individual poems retell occurrences, they can be seen as being narratives which can be analysed accordingly.

7. Summary and Outlook

Traditional texts and hypertexts are not fundamentally different - actually they have more in common than is commonly assumed and thus can be analysed well within the parameters of established categories of literary theory. I repeat my statement from the introduction of this dissertation in order to underline this fact and to show that we are now in a position to argue against early theorists of hypertext.

After having clarified our understanding of textuality, we discussed that hypertexts (and the internet) constitute a new literary genre, although because of the various instances of intertextuality these texts can best be described as belonging to a hybrid genre. Beat SUTER [87, pp. 13-14] suggests in this respect:

> Dass ein Medium ein neues Genre erzeugt, ist nichts ungewöhnliches, eher schon eine Begleiterscheinung der medialen Auseinandersetzung: Das Radio erzeugte das Hörspiel, das Kino den Spielfilm und das Fernsehen beispielsweise die Serien und die Krimis. Ob nun die Verfasser der Hyperfiktionen die Avantgarde der Literatur von morgen sind, die nach Erscheinungsmöglichkeiten literarischer Gestaltungs- und Ausdrucksformen mit neuen Mitteln sucht, oder die Arrièregarde der Literatur von gestern [...], die bekannte und bewährte Sprach- und Textspiele epigonal im neuen Medium reproduziert, der Ratlosigkeit dem Neuen gegenüber und der unsicheren Einschätzbarkeit zum Trotz lässt sich feststellen, dass hier ein neues Milieu für Literatur im Entstehen ist, das sich (nicht ganz freiwillig) ausserhalb der etablierten literarischen Welt angesiedelt hat.

In the ensuing chapter, furthermore, we have highlighted the most important technical terms and definitions of the general field of electronic literature. With regard to the latter, we have also shown which other kinds of hypertext exist both on the internet and on CD-ROMs and how hyperfiction on the internet can be located within the larger context of electronic fiction.

After that, we have seen how differently structural and semantic characteristics of hypertext are described in secondary literature stemming from various disciplines of social and literary studies. For the purpose of developing our analytical model, these characteristics - such as nonlinearity, intertextuality, and interactivity - have been closely examined and discussed against the background of hypertext.

The next step of this dissertation was to refer to an intermedial and interdisciplinary approach to narrative and the respective analytical categories, focusing on how the individual constituents of the *story/discourse*-dichotomy can be modified or expanded in order to be able the altered subject. Finally, several works of hyperfiction from the internet, bearing different characteristics and thus enabling us to highlight the most relevant facets, have undergone a close literary analysis.

The result of this analysis allows only for one conclusion: Hypertext and printed texts share many characteristics concerning their internal narrative structure as well as their literary subjects. Although the actual reading-process of a hypertext differs considerably from that of a printed text, the construction of *readings* on the side of the recipient parallels that of traditional texts. And, to put it more clearly, the senso-motoric peculiarities of accessing a piece of hyperfiction clearly do not justify a new literary paradigm in this sense. Looking at the way modern literature is received today, it is by no means true that hypertexts have overtaken printed works, on the contrary linear texts printed on paper are by far the most popular mode of distribution, both for publishers and consumers. The novel is still the mostly widely read (and for that reason, the most often purchased) form of writing that exists today. Apart from postmodern experiments, the largest audience is still quite happy with an author who is very much alive and has an interesting story to tell. Interestingly, from the analysis of works such as *The Unknown* (cf. Chapter 6.2), it becomes obvious that there is also a large amount of self-awareness (and self-criticism) in the area of hypertext writing.

7. Summary and Outlook

In summary it can be said that internet hyperfiction has not, up to this point, produced authors or playwrights like SHAKESPEARE, DICKENS or (James) JOYCE. Or, to quote ROTERMUND:

> Er ist im Netz der Netze noch nicht aufgetaucht, der Online-"Ulysses". Das hypermediale Großwerk, das seinen staunenden Lesern, Betrachtern und Hörern 24 Stunden Erlebniszeit anbietet und abzwingt. Das alle Alltagsgeschäfte und physischen Bedürfnisse ebenso vergessen läßt wie das Tränen der Augen vor dem leise flimmernden Bildschirm und das Ticken des Zählers bei der Telekom. Ein Werk, von dessen Existenz vielleicht anfänglich nur eine Gemeinde von Spezialisten weiß, das dann aber mit großem Getöse alle Feuilletons loben, preisen, sezieren und bekämpfen.[1]

The kind of specialised writing we have dealt with so far is still quite young. There are a lot of experiments, and these works seem to be made for an academic and artistic elite, who see the potential of networked writing and try to promote these works. Potentially, publication on the internet opens up an enormous target audience. Everybody all over the globe, with a computer and an internet-connection, can read what has been published just seconds ago - and thousands of miles away. In its fifteenth year of existence, the internet has developed an enormous creative potential based on a large number or participants of an information network very sensitive to global political and social developments. A comprehensive study of hypertext in this new medium, as we have seen, has to account for this networked structure. Of course, critics have convincingly argued that without editorship, the quality of artistic productions of the modern internet is lagging behind the quality which is assured by critical reading and selection and subsequent printing. However, in my opinion there are mostly economic reasons for this: writers on the web mostly produce their works as a hobby. If a way would be found to enable writers to write full-time, greater craftsmanship would probably develop. Of course, this on the other hand requires a readership that enjoys these texts. As is often argued in *The Unknown*, hypertextual writing is still something very special and not at

---

[1] http://www.weisses-rauschen.de/hero/97-10-laudatio.html, accessed 25.04.2005

all made for the mainstream taste.

Therefore it is true that the new technologies provide an excellent experimenting ground for new literatures. Literature produced in this manner will remain marginal for the time being and is by no means a substitute for established literatures.

Primary Literature

[1] M. AMERIKA, *Grammatron*, 1997. http://www.grammatron.com, accessed: 25.04.05.

[2] M.-K. ARNOLD AND M. DERBY, *kokura*, 1999. http://eastgate.com/Kokura/, accessed 25.04.05.

[3] M. ATAVAR, **** *[four stars]*, 1998. http://www.atavar.com/fourstars/, accessed 25.04.05.

[4] C. L. BUYOLI, *obituaries.count*, 2003. http://www.iua.upf.es/~clomeli/wartime/necro.html, accessed: 25.04.05.

[5] L. CARROLI AND J. WILSON, **water always writes in *plural*, 1998. http://www.hypertxt.com/sh/hyper98/water/, accessed 25.04.05.

[6] DLSAN, *IN MEMORY DO WE TRUST?*, 2003. http://www.dlsan.org/verona/, accessed: 25.04.05.

[7] C. FISHER, *These Waves of Girls*, 2001. http://www.yorku.ca/caitlin/waves/, accessed: 25.04.05.

[8] GENIWATE, *Rice*, 1998. http://www.idaspoetics.com.au/rice/riceheading.html, accessed 25.04.05.

[9] W. GILLESPIE AND S. R. ET AL., *The Unknown*, unknown date of publication. http://www.unknownhypertext.com/, accessed: 25.04.05.

Primary Literature

[10] S. HAMILL, ed., *Poets Against The War*, Thunder's Mouth Press/Nation Books, New York, 2003.

[11] M. JOYCE, *afternoon - a story (CD-ROM)*, Eastgate Systems Inc., Watertown, MA, 1987.

[12] O. LIALINA, *My Boyfriend Came Back From The War*, 1996. http://www.teleportacia.org/war/war.html, accessed 25.04.05.

[13] MISC. AUTHORS, *Project Gutenberg*, 1971-. http://www.gutenberg.net, accessed: 25.04.05.

[14] ——, *the wartime project*, 2003. http://offline.area3.net/wartime/, accessed: 25.04.05.

[15] S. MOULTHROP, *Victory Garden (CD-ROM)*, Wastgate Systems Inc, Watertown, MA, 1992.

[16] S. STRICKLAND, *The Ballad of Sand and Harry Soot*, 1999. http://www.wordcircuits.com/gallery/sandsoot/home.html, accessed 25.04.05.

Secondary Literature

[17] E. J. AARSETH, *Nonlinearity and Literary Theory*, in Hyper/Text/Theory, G. P. Landow, ed., The Johns Hopkins University Press, Baltimore and London, 1994, pp. 51–86.

[18] ——, *Cybertext - Perspectives on Ergodic Literature*, The Johns Hopkins Unversity Press, Baltimore and London, 1997.

[19] M. AMERIKA, *ÜBER GRAMMATRON*, 1997. http://www.kat.ch/alilum/3046.html/, accessed 25.04.05.

[20] M. ATAVAR, ***** [four stars]*, 1998. http://www.atavar.com/fourstars/, accessed 25.04.05.

[21] M. BAL, *Narratology - Introduction to the Theory of Narrative*, University of Toronto Press, Toronto and Buffalo and London, 1995.

[22] R. BARTHES, *The Rustle of Languages*, Hill and Wang, New York, 2nd ed., 1986, ch. The Death of the Author.

[23] D. M. BOJE, *Intertextuality Analysis - Qualitative Methods for Management and Communication Research*, 1999. http://cbae.nmsu.edu/~dboje/qm/5_intertextuality.htm, accessed: 25.04.05.

[24] J. D. BOLTER, *Writing Space - The Computer, Hypertext and the History of Writing*, Lawrence Erlbaum Associates, Hillsdale, New Jersey, 1991.

Secondary Literature

[25] Bos, Carolien van den, *Een zwervende draad*, unknown date of publication. http://www.lettertjes.net/scriptie_webbieC/, accessed 25.04.05.

[26] H.-J. Bucher, *Wie interaktiv sind die neuen Medien? Grundlagen einer Theorie der Rezeption nicht-linearer Medien*, in Die Zeitung zwischen Print und Digitalisierung, H.-J. Bucher and U. Püschel, eds., Westdeutscher Verlag, Wiesbaden, 2001, pp. 139–171.

[27] N. C. Burbules, *Rhetorics of the Web: hyperreading and critical literacy*, in Page to Screen: Taking Literacy into the Electronic Era, Ilana Snyder and M. Joyce, eds., Routledge, London, 1998, pp. 102–122.

[28] J. Caley, *The Code is not the Text (unless it is the Text)*, 2003. http://www.electronicbookreview.com/v3/servlet/ebr?essay_id=cayleyele&command=view_essay, accessed: 25.04.05.

[29] D. Chandler, *An Introduction to Genre Theory*, 1997. http://www.aber.ac.uk/media/Documents/intgenre/intgenre.html, accessed: 25.04.05.

[30] A. Chang, *consuming rice*, 2003. http://www.wordcircuits.com/comment/umd/chang.html, accessed 25.04.05.

[31] D. Charnay, *Comprehending Non-Linear Text: The Role of Discourse Cues and Reading Strategies*, in Hypertext '87 Papers, ACM, 1987, pp. 109–120.

[32] S. Chatman, *Story and Discourse. Narrative Structure in Fiction and Film,*, Cornell University Press, Ithaca and London, 1978.

[33] U. Christmann and N. G. et al., *Verarbeitungsstrategien von tradionellen (linearen) Buchtexten und zukünftigen (nicht-linearen) Hypertexten*, in Lesesozialisation in der Mediengesellschaft: Ein Schwerpunktprogramm (10. Sonderheft IASL), N. Groeben, ed., Max Niemeyer Verlag, Tübingen, 1999, pp. 175 – 189.

[34] R. Coover, *Hyperfiction: Novels for the Computer*, New York Times Book Review, (1993), pp. 8–10.

211

Secondary Literature

[35] M. DAHLSTRÖM, *When is a webtext?*, Text Technology: The Journal of Computer Text Processing, (2002), pp. 139–161.

[36] R. DE BEAUGRANDE AND W. DRESSLER, *Introduction to Text Linguistics*, Longman, London and New York, 1981.

[37] J. Y. DOUGLAS, *Understanding the Act of Reading: the WOE Beginner's Guide to Dissection*, Writing On The Edge, (1991), pp. 112–125.

[38] ——, *'How Do I Stop This Thing?': Closure and Indeterminacy in Interactive Narratives*, in Hyper/Text/Theory, G. P. Landow, ed., The Johns Hopkins University Press, Baltimore and London, 1994, pp. 159–188.

[39] J. ERNST, *'Hybride genres'*, in Metzler Lexikon Literatur- und Kulturtheorie, A. Nünning, ed., Verlag J.B. Metzler, Stuttgart, Weimar, 1998.

[40] R. O. EVANS, *'Metonomy'*, in Princeton Encyclopedia of Poetry and Poetics, A. Preminger, ed., Princeton University Press, Princeton, New Jersey, enlarged edition ed., 1974.

[41] J. FAUTH, *Poles in your face: The promises and pitfalls of hyperfiction*, 1995. http://www.mississippireview.com/1995/06-jurge.html, accessed: 25.04.05.

[42] A. GALLOWAY, *Grammatron review / Mark Amerika e-terview*, 1997. http://rhizome.org/thread.rhiz?thread=882&text=777, accessed 25.04.2005.

[43] L. GELDSETZER, *Wittgenstein's Familienähnlichkeitsbegriffe*, 1999. http://www.phil-fak.uni-duesseldorf.de/philo/geldsetzer/famaenl.htm, accessed: 25.04.05.

[44] L. D. GIANNETTI, *Understanding Movies*, Prentice-Hall, Englewood Cliffs, 2nd ed., 1976.

[45] N. GROEBEN, *Lesesozialisation in der Mediengesellschaft: Ein Schwerpunktprogramm (10. Sonderheft IASL)*, Max Niemeyer Verlag, Tübingen, 1999.

Secondary Literature

[46] F. INTEMANN, *Kommunikation, Hypertext, Design: Eine Untersuchung zur Struktur und Optimierung hypermedialer Lernumgebungen*, Waxmann, Münster, 2002.

[47] W. ISER, *The Implied Reader: Patterns of Communication in Prose Fiction from Bunyan to Beckett*, The Johns Hopkins University Press, 1974, ch. The Reading Process: A Phenomenological Approach.

[48] M. JAHN, *Narratology: A Guide to the Theory of Narrative. Part III of Poems, Plays, and Prose: A Guide to the Theory of Literary Genres*, 2003. http://www.uni-koeln.de/~ame02/pppn.htm, accessed 25.04.05.

[49] E.-M. JAKOBS, *Textvernetzung in den Wissenschaften. Zitat und Verweis als Ergebnis reproduktiven und produktiven Handelns*, Max Niemeyer Verlag, Tübingen, 1999.

[50] N. F. JENSEN, *Internet Hyperfiction. Can it ever Become a Widely Popular Artform?*, 2001. http://hjem.wanadoo.dk/~wan06376/NiJeSpeciale.htm, accessed 25.04.05.

[51] C. J. KEEP, *The Disturbing Liveliness of Machines. Rethinking the Body in Hypertext Theory and Fiction*, in Cyberspace Textuality: Computer Technology and Literary Theory, M.-L. Ryan, ed., Indiana University Press, Bloomington and Indianapolis, 1999, pp. 164–181.

[52] R. KENDALL AND N. TRAENKNER, *Charting the Frontier: The Electronic Literature Directory*, 2003. http://hypertext.rmit.edu.au/dac/papers/Kendall.pdf, accessed: 25.04.05.

[53] S. KIERNAN, *Unconscious Symbolic Strength: 'Rice' by Geniwate*, 2003. http://www.dotlit.qut.edu.au/reviews/rice.html, accessed 25.04.05.

[54] J. KRISTEVA, *Bachtin, das Wort, der Dialog und der Roman*, in Literaturwissenschaft und Linguistik. Ergebnisse und Perspektiven. Bd. 3: Zur linguistischen Basis der Literaturwissenschaft II, J. Ihwe, ed., Athenäum, Frankfurt/M, 1972, pp. 345–375.

Secondary Literature

[55] G. P. LANDOW, *Hypertext 2.0 - The Convergence of Critical Theory and Technology*, The John Hopkins University Press, Baltimore, London, 1997.

[56] J. LEY, *On Gold and Silver Ages and the Elements of Hypertext*, 2000. http: //www.pifmagazine.com/vol32/c_ley.shtml, accessed 25.04.05.

[57] G. LIESTØL, *Wittgenstein, Genette, and the Reader's Narrative*, in Hyper/Text/Theory, G. P. Landow, ed., The Johns Hopkins University Press, Baltimore and London, 1994, pp. 87–120.

[58] D. LORENZ, *Mark Amerika erfindet Literatur im Internet neu. Der Cyberschreiber und sein Golem*, Die Zeit, (16/1998). http://zeus.zeit.de/text/archiv/1998/ 16/amerika.txt.19980408.xml, accessed 25.04.2005.

[59] J. LYE, *Narrative point of view: some considerations*, 2002. http://www.brocku. ca/english/courses/2F55/pt_of_view.html, accessed 25.04.05.

[60] S. MCCLOUD, *Understanding Comics - The invisible art*, Harper Perennial, New York, 1993.

[61] A. MEDOSCH, *Das letzte Museum der Netzkunst hat eröffnet*, 2000. http://www. heise.de/tp/r4/artikel/3/3502/1.html, accessed 25.04.05.

[62] J. MILLER, *Why Hyperfiction Didn't Work*, 2001. http://reviews. media-culture.org.au/features/interactive/jmiller-c.html, accessed: 25.04.05.

[63] E. MÜLLER-ZETTELMANN, *Lyrik und Narratologie*, in Erzähltheorie transgenerisch, intermedial, interdisziplinär, A. Nünning and V. Nünning, eds., WVT, Trier, 2002, pp. 129–154.

[64] T. H. NELSON, *Literary Machines*, self-published, Swathmore, Pennsylvania, 1987.

[65] A. NÜNNING AND V. NÜNNING, eds., *Erzähltheorie transgenerisch, intermedial, interdisziplinär*, WVT, Trier, 2002.

Secondary Literature

[66] ——, *Produktive Grenzüberschreitungen: Transgenerische, intermediale und inter-disziplinäre Ansätze in der Erzähltheorie*, in Erzähltheorie transgenerisch, interme-dial, interdisziplinär, A. Nünning and V. Nünning, eds., WVT, Trier, 2002, pp. 1–22.

[67] S. ONEGA AND J. LANDA, eds., *Narratology: An Introduction*, Longman, London, New York, 1996.

[68] S. POROMBKA, *Hypertext. Zur Kritik eines digitalen Mythos*, Wilhelm Fink Verlag, München, 1999.

[69] A. RAU, *What you click is what you get? Die Stellung von Autoren und Lesern in interaktiver digitaler Literatur*, dissertation.de, Berlin, 2000.

[70] S. RIMMON-KEANAN, *Narrative Fiction. Contemporary Poetics*, Methuen, London and New York, 1983.

[71] J.-F. ROUET AND J. J. LEVONEN, *Studying and Learning With Hypertext: Em-pirical Studies and Their Implications*, in Hypertext and Cognition, J.-F. Rouet and J. J. Levonen, eds., Erlbaum, 1996.

[72] M.-L. RYAN, ed., *Cyberspace Textuality: Computer Technology and Literary The-ory*, Indiana University Press, Bloomington and Indianapolis, 1999.

[73] ——, *Narrative as Virtual Reality: Immersion and Interactivity in Literature and Electronic Media*, Parallax Series, John Hopkins University Press, Baltimore, 2001.

[74] D. SCHMAUKS, *'Deixis'*, in Metzler Lexikon Literatur- und Kulturtheorie, A. Nünning, ed., Verlag J.B. Metzler, Stuttgart, Weimar, 1998.

[75] H. SCHMUNDT, *Hyperfiction: The Romanticism of the Information Revolution*, Southern Humanities Review, (1995), pp. 309–321.

[76] K. SEIBEL, *Cyberage-Narratologie: Erzähltheorie und Hyperfiktion*, in Erzähltheorie transgenerisch, intermedial, interdisziplinär, A. Nünning and V. Nünning, eds., WVT, Trier, 2002, pp. 217–236.

[77] S. SHAVIRO, *Grammatron*, unknown date of publication. `http://plaza.bunka.` `go.jp/bunka/museum/kikaku/exhibition10/english/ie/grammatron2/index.` `html`, accessed: 25.04.05.

[78] M. SHUMATE, *Hyperizons*, unknown date of publication. `http://www.duke.edu/` `~mshumate/hyperizons/index.html`, accessed 25.04.05.

[79] R. SIMANOWSKI, *Interview with Mark Amerika: network (h)activity*, 2000. `http:` `//www.dichtung-digital.com/Interviews/Amerika-3-Nov-00/index2.htm`, accessed 25.04.05.

[80] ——, *Hypertext. Merkmale, Forschung, Poetik*, 2002. `http://www.` `dichtung-digital.org/2002/07-31-Simanowski.htm`, accessed: 25.04.05.

[81] ——, *Interfictions - Vom Schreiben im Netz*, Suhrkamp, Frankfurt am Main, 2002.

[82] I. SNYDER, *Beyond the hype: reassessing hypertext*, in Page to Screen: Taking Literacy into the Electronic Era, Ilana Snyder and M. Joyce, eds., Routledge, London, 1998, pp. 125–143.

[83] F. K. STANZEL, *Textual Power in (Short) Short Story and Poem*, in Modes of Narrative: Approaches to American, Canadian and British Fiction, R. Nischik and B. Korte, eds., Königshausen & Neumann, Würzburg, 1990, pp. 20–30.

[84] A. STORRER, *Was ist 'hyper' am Hypertext?*, 2000. `http://www.` `hytex.uni-dortmund.de/storrer/papers/hyper.pdf`, accessed: 25.04.05, PDF-Preprint.

[85] ——, *Coherence in text and hypertext*, 2002. `http://www.hytex.uni-dortmund.` `de/hytex/Publikationen/as-paper.pdf`, accessed: 25.04.05, PDF-Preprint.

[86] ——, *Neue Medien - neue Stilfragen. Das World Wide Web unter stilistischer Perspektive*, unknown date of publication. `http://www.hytex.info`, accessed: 20.01.04, PDF-Preprint.

[87] B. SUTER, *Hyperfiktion und interaktive Narration im frühen Entwicklungsstadium zu einem literarischen Genre*, update verlag, Zürich, 1999.

[88] K. WENZ, *Verschiebungen und Transformationen. Mark Amerikas 'Grammatron'*, 1999. `http://www.netzliteratur.net/wenz/wenz_amerika.htm`, accessed 25.04.05.

[89] P. WENZEL, *Der Text und seine Analyse*, in Ein anglistischer Grundkurs: Einführung in die Literaturwissenschaft, B. Fabian, ed., Erich Schmidt, Berlin, 8. Auflage ed., 1998.

[90] ——, *'Gattung, literarische', 'Gattungsgeschichte', 'Gattungstheorie und Gattungspoetik'*, in Metzler Lexikon Literatur- und Kulturtheorie, A. Nünning, ed., Verlag J.B. Metzler, Stuttgart, Weimar, 1998.

[91] ——, *Zu den übergreifenden Modellen des Erzähltextes*, in Einführung in die Erzähltextanalyse, P. Wenzel, ed., WVT, Trier, 2004, pp. 4–22.

[92] G. WHALLEY, *'Metaphor'*, in Princeton Encyclopedia of Poetry and Poetics, A. Preminger, ed., Princeton University Press, Princeton, New Jersey, enlarged edition ed., 1974.

[93] U. WIRTH, *Wen kümmert's, wer spinnt?*, in Hyperfiction. Hyperliterarisches Lesebuch: Internet und Literatur, B. Suter and M. Böhler, eds., Stroemfeld/Nexus, Frankfurt a.M. / Basel, 1999, pp. 29–42.

[94] G. WOLF, *The Great Library of Amazonia*, 2003. `http://www.wired.com/news/business/0,1367,60948,00.html?tw=wn_tophead_2`, accessed 25.04.05.

[95] W. WOLF, *Das Problem der Narrativität in Literatur, bildender Kunst und Musik: Ein Beitrag zu einer intermedialen Erzähltheorie*, in Neue Ansätze in der Erzähltheorie, A. Nünning and V. Nünning, eds., WVT, Trier, 2002, pp. 23–104.

[96] R. ZIEGFELD, *Interactive Fiction: A New Literary Genre?*, New Literary History, (1989), pp. 341–372.

Secondary Literature

[97] H. ZIEGLER, *When Hypertext became uncool. Notes on Power, Politics, and the Interface*, 2003. `http://www.dichtung-digital.org/2003/issue/1/ziegler/index.htm`, accessed 25.04.05.

[98] R. A. ZWAAN, *Effect of Genre Expectation on Text Comprehension*, Journal of Experimental Psychology, (1994), pp. 920–933.

A. Appendix: Sources and References

A.1. Research and General Information

- Dichtung Digital (`http://www.dichtung-digital.com/`)

- JoDI (`http://jodi.tamu.edu/`)

- Trace Online Writing Centre (`http://trace.ntu.ac.uk/`)

- First Monday (`http://firstmonday.org/`)

- ctheory (`http://www.ctheory.net/`)

- log.in read.in write.in: ODYSSEEN im NETZRAUM (`http://www.hyperfiction.de/`)

- Hypertext and Hypermedia (`http://www.cyberartsweb.org/`)

- Resource Center for Cyberculture Studies (`http://www.com.washington.edu/rccs/`)

- Fine Art Forum (`http://www.fineartforum.org`)

- Hyperfiction: Liste der Listen (`http://www.cyberfiction.ch/`)

- hyperfiction.ch: Sprungbrett ins Netz (`http://www.hyperfiction.ch/`)

- HYPER- diskurs, -fiktion, -text, -diss (`http:www.hyperdis.de`)

- Johannes Auer: Theoretische Texte zur Netzliteratur // Internetliteratur // Netzkunst (`http://www.netzliteratur.net/`)

A.2. Primary Texts

- the wartime project (`http://offline.area3.net/wartime/`)

- Drunken Boat (`http://www.drunkenboat.com/`)

- sidereality (`http://www.sidereality.com/`)

- Rhizome (`http://www.rhizome.com/`)

- Eastgate (`http://www.eastgate.com/`)

- Webartery (`http://www.webartery.com/defib/webarterymembers.htm\`)

- G V O O N (`http://www.gvoon.de`)

- Electronic Literature Directory (`http://directory.eliterature.org/`)

- Hyperizons (`http://www.duke.edu/~mshumate/hyperfic.html`)

- electronic poetry center (`http://epc.buffalo.edu/`)

A.3. Typology according to the ELD

Hypertext (poetry/fiction/drama/nonfiction) Ted Nelson, who coined the term, defines "hypertext" as "non-sequential writing – text that branches and allows choices to the reader." It is usually implemented as chunks of text connected by links, though other forms of nonlinear writing have also come to be recognized as hypertext. For our purposes, we do not consider a linear series of pages linked together to be hypertext. Nor do we consider links added to a conventional table of contents to constitute hypertext.

Reader Collaboration (poetry/fiction/drama/nonfiction) Work that allows readers to add their own writing to the text, which then becomes a permanent part of the work. A reader's additions are stored on the work's Web site or, in the case of disk-based work, on the reader's hard disk.

A. Appendix: Sources and References

Recorded Reading/Performance (poetry/fiction/drama/nonfiction) Digitized audio or video of a text being read or performed aloud, usually by its author. This category contains mostly poetry.

Animated Text (poetry/fiction/drama/nonfiction) Work using animated text (also known as kinetic text) in which words move or morph onscreen. This category contains mostly poetry.

Other Audio/Video/Animation (poetry/fiction/drama/nonfiction) Work using audio, video, or animation in ways not covered by one of the categories above. Individual listings distinguish between audio and video/animation, though these are combined as a single browsing category for user convenience.

Prominent Graphics (poetry/fiction/drama/nonfiction) Work in which graphics and visual elements play a significant role, such as visual poetry.

Generated Text (poetry/fiction/drama/nonfiction) Texts created in real time by software that uses rules and random processes for combining words. Each time the work is viewed, a different text is generated. This category excludes work that does not contain text-generating code but consists merely of nonvariable text produced by a separate text-generating program.

A.4. Structural Typology according to Suter

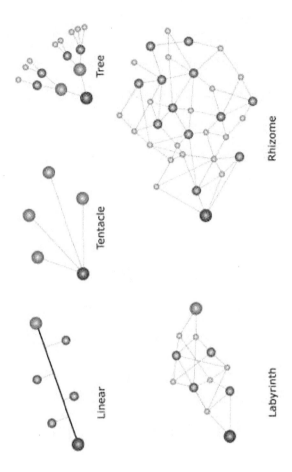

A.5. 'Zweiebenenmodell mit ausgestalteter Diskursebene'

[91]

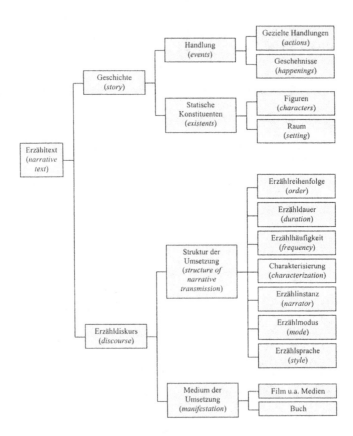

Bildungsgang des Verfassers

Name Roman Zenner

Geburtsdatum 26. Juli 1977

Geburtsort Würselen bei Aachen, NRW

Allgemeine Hochschulreife Städtisches Gymnasium Übach-Palenberg, 1996

Studium
- 10/1996 - 07/2001 RWTH Aachen (Anglistische Literaturwissenschaft, Anglistische Sprachwissenschaft, Volkswirtschaftslehre)
- 09/1998 - 07/1999 University of Reading, GB
- 02/2000 - 12/2000 University of Western Australia, Perth

Mündliche Doktorprüfung 2. Mai 2005

www.ingramcontent.com/pod-product-compliance
Lightning Source LLC
LaVergne TN
LVHW022308060326
832902LV00020B/3348